HUKA LODGE
DESSERTS

RECIPES BY GREG HEFFERNAN
PHOTOGRAPHS BY JOHN PETTITT

Published by Huka Lodge

PUBLISHING CO-ORDINATOR: Donna Hoyle
EDITOR: Alison Dench
ART DIRECTION AND STYLING: Donna Hoyle
PHOTOGRAPHY: John Pettitt
DINNERWARE FOR PHOTOGRAPHY: The Studio of Tableware and Tessuti
FABRICS: Unique Fabrics
PAINT FINISHES: Juliet Bamford
JACKET AND BOOK DESIGN: Donna Hoyle
FINISHED ARTWORK: Michelle Tack
TYPESETTING: Jazz Graphics
SEPARATIONS AND PLATES: Hang Ngai Arts Co.
PRINTING AND BINDING: Everbest Printing Co. Ltd.

Published by Huka Lodge,
P.O. Box 6993, Auckland, New Zealand.
Distributed in New Zealand by
Hodder & Stoughton Ltd, 46 View Road,
Glenfield, Auckland.
Distributed in Australia by
Simon & Schuster Australia,
20 Barcoo Street, East Roseville, NSW 2069.
Copyright © 1993 Huka Lodge:
Greg Heffernan (recipes) and
John Pettitt (photographs)
First published 1993
ISBN 0-473-01830-6

Printed in Hong Kong

ACKNOWLEDGEMENTS

A s the owner of Huka Lodge, I wish to extend my personal thanks to the following people, whose contributions to *Huka Lodge Desserts* have been invaluable.

Greg Heffernan, our Executive Chef, has shown continuing dedication, putting in the extra effort this project required, and his wife, Julie, has again given her support. John Pettitt has captured our cuisine at its finest with his magnificent photographs and Donna Hoyle has again brought her special qualities of design, planning and creativity to the production of this book. Michael Brajkovich, Master of Wine, has shared his interest in dessert wines with great depth and knowledge. Geoffrey Martin wrote the essays 'Around the Great Lake' and 'One of the World's Special Places' so skilfully for our first book and has given permission for them to appear again. Martin Keay wrote the essay describing the designs and themes he has woven into our beautiful gardens.

Finally, to our staff who have all contributed in many ways to help create a book we can all be proud of, my thanks.

Alexander van Heeren

CONTENTS

FOREWORD

Welcome to the sequel to *Huka Lodge's Cook Book*. Little did I know that the success of our first publishing venture would mean that a companion volume would appear so soon. Whilst our first cook book primarily featured the Lodge's famed fish and game menus, comments made by guests and friends suggested it would be timely and appropriate to devote an entire book to our desserts. At Huka Lodge desserts represent creative flair and artistry; they are visually exciting and create new taste sensations.

The choice of desserts at the Lodge is both extensive and varied, so we had to consider carefully not what to include, but rather what to leave out. You will not, I am sure, be disappointed by our selection. I do hope you will be able to visit Huka Lodge and enjoy these desserts for yourself. If, for reasons of time and distance, you cannot visit us in the near future, we have come to you within the pages of this book.

We hope you enjoy *Huka Lodge Desserts*. As with our previous cook book, it has been a labour of love by all concerned. At Huka Lodge, that's the way things are.

Alexander van Heeren

Huka Lodge, nestled among the trees on the banks of the Waikato River.

AROUND THE GREAT LAKE

Lake Taupo lies at the very heart of New Zealand's North Island, more than three hundred metres above sea-level. The lake is guarded to the south by a trilogy of snow-capped mountains and to the north, beyond rolling hills and vast, fragrant pine forests, are the geysers and the fumaroles of the Rotorua thermal area.

Your first impression of Lake Taupo will be one of peaceful beauty. You will have been deceived because the origins of the region and its lake are violent.

Little more than two thousand years ago an eruption of gigantic proportions took place. The explosions sent a shower of ash scattering for a radius of nearly one hundred miles.

The crater eventually began to fill with water and, according to the legend of the Maori people of the Tuwharetoa Tribe, Taupo Moana — the Sea of Taupo — was born. Filled by ice-cold rivers flowing from the mountains that rim the lake, Lake Taupo is crystal clear and breathtakingly cold.

At the northern tip a strong river leaves the lake on a three hundred kilometre journey to the sea. The Waikato is New Zealand's longest river. After a tortuous infancy, it thunders over a series of rapids that eventually become the Huka Falls. Their beauty will astound you, the deep aquamarine hue amaze you. These falls are nature at her theatrical best.

The Waikato River below the Lodge before cascading over the falls.   CRAIG POTTON

The main Lodge at twilight.

Almost hidden in the trees above the falls is Huka Lodge, considered to occupy the most beautiful position of any lodge in the world. From here every nook and cranny of the Taupo region can be explored.

And there is much to do. The lake offers the best rainbow trout fishing in the world. For the skier, Mount Ruapehu has the longest runs on spring snow in the Southern Hemisphere. The mountains to the east provide hundreds of square kilometres of subalpine wilderness where deer and trout are the quarry of a dedicated fraternity of hunters and fishermen.

No matter what pursuit brings you to Taupo, you will do it in an environment that is pure and clean. You will be in a place where the air is so clear you can see for a hundred kilometres; where the seasons are so well defined as to appear carefully sketched.

Taupo's spring heralds the end of sharp winter snow winds, cracking frosts and runs of trout up tumbling rivers to spawn at the place of their own birth.
The summers are hot and the tussock of distant hills is parched by dry winds.
Our autumn? The leaf-change is so vivid that it sends splashes of gold running down the river valleys.

All of which seems to happen in homage to the Great Lake.

ABOVE: From left, Mt Ruapehu, the cone of Mt Ngauruhoe and the flat peak of Mt Tongariro, seen from the Taupo township foreshore. BELOW: The Boat Harbour, Lake Taupo.

ONE OF THE WORLD'S SPECIAL PLACES

What is the magic of Huka Lodge? And why is it considered to be one of the greatest lodges of the world? The clue to the answer possibly lies in one word: uniqueness.

Since its formal restoration in 1985, Huka Lodge has enjoyed a renaissance which has once again given it world fame. Something that tends to overshadow its simple beginnings when a young man first claimed its site by the edge of a remote Taupo river.

Alan Pye was a man whose eye could not conceal a glint. He led everyone to believe that he was Irish yet that has never been established. How he arrived in New Zealand or who first employed him also remains a mystery.

Alan Pye, founder of Huka Lodge.

Pye's itinerant life changed when his love of fishing brought him to Taupo in the mid-twenties. In those days, Taupo was isolated and the journey from anywhere was regarded as a trek. Yet Taupo's fame as an angler's paradise was already established. Zane Grey had told the world of his massive catches on the Tongariro and already smaller lodges had begun to dot the lake's eastern shoreline.

But it was the mighty Waikato that lured Pye. The river had a peerless reputation for its dry fly fishing. Each day, like clockwork, sedge fly would hatch from rafts of vivid green weed beneath the river's surface. Knowing that the river was popular with fly fishermen who were prepared to make the long trip, Pye decided to procure land on its banks and build a lodge.

The origins of Huka Lodge were humble, to say the least. Anglers were accommodated in huts with slatted floors. On each a stout wooden frame was draped with heavy canvas. Anglers slept here and joined Pye and his wife in the main lodge room for generous drinks and meals of ample proportion. Such was the Pyes' hospitality that the fame of Huka Lodge spread to every corner of the angling world. The quality of the fly fishing almost began to take second place to the conviviality and atmosphere the Lodge created.

Alan Pye fishing from the bank of the Waikato River.

The original canvas huts *circa* 1935.

By the mid-1930s, Pye's fame was at its peak. Flies had been tied and named after him. A New York angling club bore his name and the Lodge's visitors' book was silent testimony to its international reputation. The following names appeared: Her Royal Highness The Duchess of York, Charles E. Lindbergh, James A. Michener (who wrote part of *Return to Paradise* at the Lodge), as well as Governors-General and many famous film stars and politicians.

Things had never looked better for the Lodge. Then war came, and with it went the mobility of its international guests. At the same time, changes took place in the river itself. After the control gates were installed on the river at Taupo, water levels became too erratic for the delicate sedge and the fishing as a consequence diminished in value.

Of course, Pye's loyal patrons continued to come, but the emphasis moved to the lake and its rivers. This probably means that Pye could be called Taupo's first and foremost angling guide.

With advancing age, Pye's involvement decreased. He died in 1973 at Taupo, an international identity who will never be forgotten. Alan Pye's main legacy is that of personal hospitality and that is the cornerstone of the Lodge today.

Without doubt, the Lodge's location is unique in itself. Set in seven private hectares, with wide sweeps of lawn running up from the river, Huka Lodge is one of those few places that establishes its charm immediately with its guests. Redwoods tower above its wooden shingle roof and the very architecture of the Lodge suggests that it is at one with its environment. Now, instead of canvas-framed sleeping quarters, a series of lavish individual lodges house guests. Each lodge is nestled in native trees and faces directly on to the river.

The guest lodges at Huka Lodge.

It was not like this when the present owner, Alex van Heeren, bought the property. His goal was to recreate the ambience of the early days of the Lodge by gathering a group of individually talented people who were as motivated as he.

He needed an architect who could identify with the Lodge's past, present and future, to provide designs that would contribute to its unique character; builders who could translate design into reality — who saw materials as a medium of expression and whose craftsmanship would stand the test of time. He sought a landscape gardener to enrich the contours of these perfect hectares and to plant trees to enhance the already beautiful environment. He needed an interior designer who believed that any form of ostentation is distasteful.

Once he found his team, van Heeren told them of his expectations. They in turn expected much of him. They persuaded and cajoled until their ideas were accepted.

The result in terms of interior design is one of eclectic and ambient charm. The designer, Virginia Fisher, never lost sight of the fact that Huka Lodge is a country lodge. She skilfully combined antique Georgian country furniture imported from Europe with solid and comfortable pieces made locally.

The paintings at Huka Lodge are a delight to behold. Some are 17th Century

European, some are local. Each work has been chosen for its fish or game theme. Scattered throughout the Lodge, sometimes in the most unexpected places, you will find the Lodge's discreet tartan motif.

Informed opinion describes the design of Huka Lodge as possessing a rare quality, that of understated taste executed with style and flair.

The Lodge Room, where guests gather for pre-dinner drinks.

The main Lodge is the centre of activity. Here guests gather to dine, meet guides and, over pre-dinner drinks, regale each other with the events of the day: of river, lake, court and course.

Staff members go out of their way to provide superb low-key service and ensure that guests enjoy their time at the Lodge. Never obtrusive, they make a point of arranging anything a guest requires. It may be fishing guides for fly angling on Taupo's rivers, a cruise on the Lodge's own high-speed vessel, *Prime Time*, to the Western Bays for a spot of armchair angling or a picnic, helicopter flights to the

Luncheon is casual at Huka Lodge — either a picnic while out fishing or dining on the terrace.

wilderness, horse trekking, a few rounds of golf on Wairakei's world-rated course or just a few fresh tennis balls for a couple of quick sets on the Lodge's own court.

In an increasingly impersonal world, the service and aura of Huka Lodge remain the essence of its charm. Perhaps this is why the respected Relais et Châteaux organisation awarded Huka Lodge its prestigious Yellow Shield, the only such award made in New Zealand. Its criteria? That a Lodge should offer the highest standards of character, courtesy, calm, comfort and cuisine.

This spirit of excellence has meant that the Lodge has found itself in a world spotlight on many occasions. Andrew Harper, the noted United States travel writer, said: 'In a country not known for its epicurean cuisine, Huka Lodge reigns supreme.' In Lord Lichfield's *Courvoisier's Book of the Best* appears the comment: 'My favourite holiday place in the world is Huka Lodge in Taupo. It is equal to the best five star accommodation in the world.'

Further international acclaim came when Huka Lodge was chosen as the venue for the 1987 GATT Conference on Tariffs and Trade. Ministers from 24 member nations spent two days at the Lodge for one of the most important conferences of its kind in recent years.

The Lodge has become the retreat of royalty and several crowned heads in European Houses have visited Huka Lodge for a brief sojourn in a round of hectic duties. Television crews have visited the Lodge to film sequences for such programmes as *Lifestyles of the Rich and Famous*.

Huka Lodge is now a tribute to the foresight of Alex van Heeren, the businessman who came here and saw the potential of the Lodge and its site. In the Queen's honours list of 1988, Alex van Heeren was made an Honorary Member of the Order of the British Empire for his services to tourism and exports. He divides his time between various business interests and his role as Honorary Consul of the Netherlands in Auckland.

Just as Alan Pye shaped the Lodge's past, Alex van Heeren plotted its future. Yet some things about Huka Lodge will never change. Its magic is ever-present. As present as the river mists that greet each guest every morning as if to remind them that this river will flow forever.

THE GARDENS AT HUKA LODGE

S et against a magnificent backdrop of trees and framed by the swiftly flowing Waikato River, the Lodge gardens provide year-round interest and beauty. Old photographs of the area show a barren and largely treeless landscape, but the foresight of past owners in planting now-mature pines, redwoods and firs has created a strong base for the recent development of the gardens.

View of stream garden, with gunnera, irises and hostas.

Those existing trees have been added to with a variety of exotic and native species, with the emphasis on large informal shrubberies giving concentrated spring interest, and on broad plantings of annuals and perennials to provide colour and foliage effect over the summer months. Several years' growth has enhanced the feeling of maturity, with hundreds of daffodils planted in simple drifts around trees giving the earliest colour in the year. Shrubs such as rhododendrons, spiraea, magnolias, dogwoods and philadelphus, which take several years to settle down to regular flowering, provide colour in spring while form and foliage remain interesting for the rest of the summer.

The focus of the garden as a whole is the stream garden, which features gunnera, hosta, iris, astilbe and primulas. These moisture-loving plants have grown into bold drifts where previously small clumps existed, as a result of natural increase and division. October to December are the peak months for display here, followed by a mixture of traditional perennials and annuals for the rest of summer, in a scheme of white, blue and yellow.

No garden remains static for long and at Huka Lodge there have been major improvements and additions. Extensive planting continues, adding plants in larger and simpler colours, discarding poor growers and less effective varieties. Original plantings of a sometimes short-term nature have made way for new material that creates a more homogeneous landscape. A timber-shingled summer house forms the focus of the main gardens while framing the view of the distant Huka Falls and the beautifully coloured water. The river bank has been cleared behind this to expose rock faces and paths, and subtle lighting adds interest to this backdrop at night.

Vegetable and herb gardens provide produce for the kitchen, while a bed of cutting flowers supplements florists' flowers for most of the year. The tennis court nearby is screened by a cyprus hedge, turning this corner of the garden into a setting for outside events, with the adjacent enclosed lawns allowing for summer seating.

Seasonal colour is a feature of the Lodge terrace, all-round interest in planters being achieved by seasonal annuals, and the highlight of massed tulips bulbs in spring. Scarlet cyclamen and impatiens in pots at the front doors provide welcoming colour for months on end.

The landscape at Huka Lodge has been designed as a series of gardens set amongst the seven-hectare grounds. Surrounded by such inspiring natural beauty, they are special places for leisurely garden strolls, privacy, peace and quiet.

Iceland poppy.

Gunnera tinctoria.

Leaves of *Hosta fortunei* 'Albo-picta'.

Tulips underplanted with blue pansies.

DESSERT WINES

Sweet wines may be back in style, but even now many people, while enjoying the occasional dessert wine, simply do not take sweet wine seriously. It is their loss: a quality dessert wine is one of the pinnacles of the winemaker's craft. I am convinced that, if asked to nominate a single 'desert island wine', the vast majority of winemakers would select one of the great sweet wines.

Many wine consumers begin their interest by drinking some of the ubiquitous medium-sweet wines, which may be enjoyed equally with or without food. These are generally wines of good quality but without any great merit. Tastes change, however, and as the wine drinker becomes more experienced he or she may begin to enjoy a glass or two of more serious, drier wine with a meal. This is perfectly reasonable, but to these people 'sweet' may not now equal 'serious'. They are sadly mistaken and are missing out on one of the great pleasures of the wine world.

Sweet wines are, needless to say, high in sugar; they have been made from grapes that have undergone a form of concentration, leading to a higher than normal sugar content. This often means that their alcohol content, body, richness and flavour are greater, too. It is, however, the overriding sweetness that allows these wines to be matched with dessert dishes, giving them their New Zealand name. In England the description 'pudding wine' is often heard, whereas in Australia sweet wine styles are sometimes referred to as 'stickies'.

Matching wine with food is an interesting exercise. It may be relatively simple, such as with light entrées and main courses, or quite complex, as with gamey meats or strong cheeses. Choosing an appropriate wine for a dessert is always difficult, principally because of the high sugar content of both the wine and the food. If one has more sugar than the other, then they will be mismatched; acidity, alcohol and flavour must also be balanced. Dessert wines have some quite distinct and concentrated flavours, and these may be either strong or delicate; the food accompanying such wine should be similar in the intensity of these characteristics to prevent either the wine or the food dominating.

Sauternes and its close neighbour Barsac are perhaps the most famous and highly regarded of the dessert wine styles. Made from Sémillon and Sauvignon grapes grown in the southern reaches of the Bordeaux region around the River Ciron, these wines are regarded by many as the epitome of sweet white wines. The secret of their production is the fungus *Botrytis cinerea*, which causes the famous 'noble rot' that first infects then slowly dehydrates the berries and concentrates their contents. This results in juice of high sugar, acid and flavour, which then ferments slowly to produce a sweet wine of relatively high alcohol and amazing richness and complexity. The mould also adds its own distinctive citrus/honey-like bouquet and flavour, a luscious and very pleasant character much prized by connoisseurs.

The most famous of all Sauternes is Château d'Yquem, which has its own unique rating in the Bordeaux classification of First Great Growth. Its immediate neighbour is the First Growth Château Suduiraut, to which it was once annexed. Both of these properties produce wines that are rich, alcoholic and full of depth and intensity. They have also had the benefit of at least two to three years' fermentation and maturation in new oak barrels, which gives even further nuances of concentration and complexity. Nearby, but on the other side of the River Garonne, are the lesser known appellations of Cérons, Loupiac and Sainte-Croix-du-Mont, which also produce high quality sweet wines at very reasonable prices.

The high acidity of botrytised sweet wines means that the food that is matched with them also needs to have a relatively high acid. Dishes incorporating fresh fruits such as strawberries, raspberries, boysenberries, lemon or oranges will all work quite well. Cream should be kept to a minimum to prevent masking the wine's piquancy and freshness. Peaches and apricots share many of the same fruit characters

and mesh nicely with these wines. Soufflés and cheesecakes, with the appropriate fruit bases, also make interesting food and wine marriages with Sauternes, and with the other styles of botrytised wines.

The Rhine and Mosel areas of Germany and the Alsace region of France also make wonderful sweet white wines that have been affected by botrytis, but with quite different varieties. Riesling, Pinot Gris (Rülander) and Gewürztraminer grapes are prevalent here, and when very ripe can make extraordinary dessert wines. Again the acid is important, but the flavours are even more citrus and floral than with the Sauternes, and the alcohol content is usually lower. This results in lighter textured and fruitier wines, usually without the added embellishments of wood ageing. The German wines of this type are normally labelled Auslese, or Beerenauslese. The richest, most concentrated wines are produced from individually selected botrytis-infected berries and are called Trockenbeerenauslese. The Marcel Deiss Gewürztraminer Vendanges Tardives is a very good example of the Alsace style, with a fuller alcohol than the German types.

In the south of France there are many sweet wines in the category of *vins doux naturels*, and a great number of these are produced from the Muscat grape. The most famous of these is Muscat de Beaumes de Venise, which is made from Muscat de Frontignan grapes and only lightly fortified with grape spirit to halt the fermentation and keep the wine sweet. It has the typically irrepressible fruitiness of Muscat and is luscious, full and soft, a good alternative to the Sauternes styles when the dish is strongly flavoured and with a lower acidity.

The Italians also produce dessert wine styles from grapes that are harvested and allowed to dry and raisin. These wines are known as Passito, or more commonly as Recioto. They include the vibrantly intense Recioto di Valpolicella and the famous golden-hued Vin Santo. They can vary somewhat in their level of sweetness, but they are always full of character and provide a superb accompaniment to many desserts.

Originally produced for the sweet tastes of Anglo-Saxon customers, and fortified with brandy to preserve them on the journey north, the wines of Sherry and Port have enjoyed immense popularity over the centuries. Portuguese Tawny Port is sweet but not cloying, and is well suited to either apéritif or dessert use. Older Tawnies such as those labelled 10 or 20 years old have the benefit of long periods of barrel maturation, which lends an aged *rancio* character that matches well with nuts and fruitcake. Australian Tawny Port is usually sweeter and more suited to very sweet and rich desserts. Vintage Ports are quite full-bodied, tannic wines that require a long period of bottle maturation. They are generally drier than the Tawny styles, and better presented with cheese or nuts rather than a very sweet dessert.

Wine styles similar to the classic Europeans are now being produced all over the New World. Tawny and Vintage Port styles have been successfully produced in California, Australia and New Zealand for many years, but more recently we have been seeing excellent examples of the sweet and extra-sweet table wines coming to

the fore. Riesling and Sémillon are the grape varieties that are showing through, with wines such as the de Bortoli Sémillon now recognised worldwide and the Heggies Riesling particularly popular in the Antipodes.

In New Zealand some good results were achieved initially with the Müller-Thurgau grape, but now it is the more classical aroma and flavour of the great Riesling variety that is producing the most outstanding wines. Careful management of the vineyards allows the grapes to hang on the vine until very late in the season and develop the 'noble rot', and a sound technological approach to fermenting the high-sugar, high-acid juice now produces sweet dessert wines of real international style and class. Numerous overseas wine judges and critics have commented on the remarkable improvement in the quality of sweet wines in New Zealand over a very short period. Yet, despite their undoubted quality, these intensely flavoured wines still command only a very small share of the market. We should all do more to redress the balance, and in the process do ourselves a great favour by treating ourselves to that marvellous synergy of fine dessert with fine dessert wine.

Michael Brajkovich
Master of Wine

AN INTRODUCTION TO THE RECIPES

Desserts play an important role in our menus at Huka Lodge. They form the final fifth course to the meal ensuring the memory often lingers beyond the dining table. The right dessert provides the balance essential to complement the dishes served previously. If we have served a hearty soup followed by a venison main course, then a light, refreshing dessert may appear. Alternatively, a light soup and a main course of baked salmon would be followed by a richer, more substantial dessert.

Desserts lend themselves to some wonderful combinations of flavours and textures and all the desserts featured in this book are currently served at Huka Lodge. We have endeavoured to include a diverse selection of desserts with varying degrees of complexity. The recipes have been compiled with a sincere desire to interest, instruct and inspire you in the creation of fine food and, most importantly, to share with you the pleasures of the dessert.

In all cases, before starting study the recipe and assemble all the necessary equipment. If you want to achieve the same results you must pay strict attention to the exact ingredients specified and in particular their quality. Substitution can well result in disappointment.

When making delicate desserts it is essential that weights and measures are exact. A good set of scales can ensure this level of accuracy is easily achieved. All figures given in brackets are conversions for the benefit of American readers — they are American ounces, fluid ounces and pints, rather than imperial measures. The teaspoon is a level 5ml teaspoon and the tablespoon a level 15ml.

Cooking times are as accurate as possible, but it is important to note that there can often be considerable variation, especially at low temperatures, from one oven to another. Always use the temperature given as a guide and keep a careful watch on any dish while baking.

In many recipes I have given background information on particular ingredients; knowing something about the ingredients I am using is essential to my culinary philosophy. I believe that this knowledge allows greater understanding and potential creativity in cooking and is the secret ingredient for success.

Great meals are often remembered for their great desserts. They may be the last on the menu but they are most certainly not the least!

Greg Heffernan
Executive Chef

CARAMELISED RICE PUDDING
WITH TROPICAL FRUIT AND PASSIONFRUIT SAUCE

For this dessert you will need short grain rice, cooked very slowly. If the rice is still slightly firm once the liquid has been absorbed, add a little more milk and continue to cook.

The variety of fruits is up to you. My favourites are pawpaw, pineapple, melon and mango. During the summer months stone fruit such as apricots, peaches and nectarines provide another good variation.

You will need six 150ml (5 fl oz) moulds for each portion. The rice pudding must be prepared the day before and allowed to firm up in the refrigerator overnight.

INGREDIENTS — SERVES 6

| 110g | (4 oz) | castor sugar |
| 200ml | (7 fl oz) | water |

PUDDING

450ml	(15 fl oz)	milk
300ml	(10 fl oz)	cream
1		vanilla pod, split
250g	(9 oz)	short grain rice
150g	(5½ oz)	castor sugar
3		egg yolks
100g	(3½ oz)	soft unsalted butter

SAUCE

		pulp of 6
		passionfruit
100ml	(3½ fl oz)	sugar syrup
		(see page 134)

FRUIT

pawpaw
pineapple
melon
mango
mint to garnish

CARAMEL: Combine the sugar and water, place over a high heat and caramelise to a deep amber. Remove from heat, cool briefly then divide evenly between the six moulds.

PUDDING: Place the milk, cream and vanilla pod in a medium-sized pot then bring to the boil. Add the rice then cook until soft over a very gentle heat for approximately 25–30 minutes. Stir regularly. Once cooked remove the vanilla and cool for 15 minutes at room temperature, stirring from time to time.

Whisk the castor sugar and egg yolks together until they turn pale yellow.

Beat the soft butter into the rice a little at a time, Add the yolks and sugar mixture and combine well using a wooden spoon.

Evenly divide the mixture between the moulds then place in the refrigerator overnight covered in plastic wrap.

SAUCE: Mix the passionfruit pulp with the sugar syrup and put aside until required.

TO SERVE: Dip the moulds in very hot water for the count of 10 then firmly shake the puddings out onto the serving plates. Tidily arrange three thin slices of pawpaw, three segments of pineapple, three medium-sized melon balls and three slices of mango on each plate then spoon over the passionfruit sauce.

Garnish with mint and serve slightly chilled.

CHOCOLATE MARQUISE WRAPPED IN TUILE

This dessert is far easier to prepare than it looks. The marquise may be made the day before and kept covered in the refrigerator, and the tuile ribbons will also keep for a day if kept dry and airtight.

You will need a 6.5cm (2½") diameter plain cutter to stamp out the chocolate discs and a 24cm x 2.75cm (9½" x 1") template cut from plastic or cardboard and a second 7cm (2¾") diameter plain cutter to form the tuile ribbons.

The tuile recipe will yield more than you require, but the mixture will keep for some time, covered in the refrigerator. The tuiles are very delicate, so it may pay to make a few extras.

INGREDIENTS — SERVES 6

125g (4½ oz)	castor sugar
3	egg yolks
80g (3 oz)	cocoa
150g (5½ oz)	soft unsalted butter
75g (2½ oz)	dark chocolate
2½ tbsp	icing sugar
250ml (8½ fl oz)	cream

TUILES

60g (2 oz)	unsalted butter
2	egg whites
110g (4 oz)	castor sugar
	pinch of salt
60g (2 oz)	flour
1 tbsp	finely chopped orange zest
	a little cocoa

COULIS

150g (5½ oz)	red berries (raspberries, strawberries)
100ml (3½ fl oz)	sugar syrup (see page 134)

GARNISH

	chocolate cigars (see page 130)
	fresh berries
	mint
	icing sugar for dusting

METHOD: In a large bowl add the castor sugar to the egg yolks then beat together until pale.

In a separate bowl beat the cocoa into the soft butter and put aside until required.

Finely chop the chocolate and place in a bowl over a pot of simmering water. Completely melt, then beat the chocolate into the egg yolks and sugar. Add the butter and cocoa to the chocolate and beat together.

Add the icing sugar to the cream and lightly whip. Mix into the chocolate.

Lay a sheet of greaseproof paper on a flat tray and evenly spread the marquise mixture to a thickness of approximately 2cm (¾"). This will give sufficient area to cut six portions of marquise. Allow to set in the refrigerator then cover with plastic wrap.

TUILES: Place all the ingredients, except the zest and cocoa, in a food processor and mix until smooth. Add the zest. Transfer to a bowl and allow to stand for 15 minutes.

If possible use a non-stick teflon sheet to line a baking tray, as this will make the process far easier. If one is not available, then liberally butter the tray then dust with flour.

Place the 24cm x 2.75cm (9½" x 1") template on the baking tray then evenly spread the tuile mixture within the shape to approximately 1mm deep.

Carefully lift the template then proceed with another one or two. Bake in batches.

Mix a little cocoa with water to a piping consistency. Carefully pipe two fine lines of cocoa paste along the length of each tuile ribbon then bake each batch in a preheated 190°C (375°F) oven for 5 minutes or until golden brown all over.

Working quickly, while the tuile is still hot, form each around the 7cm (2¾") cutter. Pinch the ends together, remove from the cutter and allow to cool and set. Handle the ribbons with care as they are very brittle.

If the tuiles cool too much and will not bend, put them back in the oven and warm through then try again. Store dry and airtight.

COULIS: Place the berries and sugar syrup in a food processor and purée until smooth. Pass through a fine sieve, cover and store in the refrigerator.

TO SERVE: Stamp out discs from the chilled marquise mixture with the 6.5cm (2½") cutter then carefully lift off the tray with a fish slice. Place on the serving plate then put a tuile ribbon around each. Scatter the berry selection around the plate then dribble over a little coulis.

Garnish with the chocolate cigars and mint, lightly dust with icing sugar and serve at room temperature.

WHISKEY CAKE WITH COFFEE SAUCE

This is a dark rich cake, lightly flavoured with whiskey and filled with chocolate ganache. Any good quality whiskey will do.

Once the cake is baked and cooled, moisten with strong whiskey-flavoured sugar syrup before adding the ganache to ensure a malty flavour.

The coffee sauce is similar to a crème anglaise and can be made a day or so in advance as it will keep well, covered, in the refrigerator.

INGREDIENTS — MAKES 1

400g	(14 oz)	flour
4 tbsp		cocoa
1 tsp		salt
1 tsp		baking powder
450g	(1 lb)	castor sugar
210ml	(7 fl oz)	walnut or sunflower oil
3-4		eggs
225ml	(7½ fl oz)	whiskey
250ml	(8½ fl oz)	milk
100g	(3½ oz)	raisins
150g	(6½ oz)	shelled walnuts, finely chopped
200ml	(7 fl oz)	sugar syrup (see page 134)
		icing sugar for dusting
		walnuts to garnish

CHOCOLATE GANACHE

200g	(7 oz)	dark chocolate
100ml	(3½ fl oz)	cream

COFFEE SAUCE

6		egg yolks
110g	(4 oz)	castor sugar
2 tsp		granulated instant coffee
450ml	(15 fl oz)	milk

METHOD: Sift the flour, cocoa, salt and baking powder together. In another bowl whisk the sugar and oil together then mix in the eggs and 125ml (4 fl oz) of the whiskey.

Stir half the milk then half the flour mixture into the sugar and eggs and combine well. Add the remaining milk then the remaining flour and combine. Mix in the raisins and chopped walnuts.

Line a 24cm (9½ ″) round or square tin with greaseproof paper or butter then dust with flour.

Pour in the cake mixture then bake in a preheated 170 °C (325 °F) for 30 minutes, with the fan on. Reduce the oven to 100 °C (210 °F) then continue to bake for a further 45 minutes with the fan on, or until a skewer inserted into the middle comes out clean. Cool for 1 hour in the tin before turning out.

Mix the sugar syrup and the rest of the whiskey together, ready for moistening the cake.

CHOCOLATE GANACHE: Chop the chocolate and melt in a bowl over a pot of simmering water.

Bring the cream to the boil then mix into the melted chocolate. Combine thoroughly. Remove from the heat and allow to cool to a spreading consistency, stirring regularly.

COFFEE SAUCE: Place the egg yolks and sugar in a bowl. Whisk together well, until the mixture doubles in volume. Add the coffee to the milk and place in a heavy-bottomed pot over a medium heat. Bring to the boil. Pour the hot milk onto the egg mixture, stirring as you go.

Return to a clean pot and place over a gentle heat, stirring constantly with a wooden spoon. On no account allow the custard to boil. Cook until it forms a coating consistency, then pass through a fine sieve into a clean bowl.

Allow to cool completely, stirring from time to time. Cover to prevent a skin forming.

TO SERVE: Cut the cake in half horizontally then liberally brush both freshly cut surfaces with the whiskey sugar syrup. Spread the chocolate ganache evenly over one side, going right to the edges, then place the other half on top and lightly press together.

Cut the cake into portions, dust with icing sugar and sprinkle with walnuts. Divide the coffee sauce evenly between each portion and serve.

COMPÔTE OF DRIED FRUITS BAKED UNDER A CINNAMON SPONGE

This is a very easy and tasty dessert. The variety of dried fruit you use is entirely up to you. We use the prepared mixed fruits available in health food shops and supermarkets then add more favourites. The cinnamon sponge is quite a durable type so it forms more of a sponge biscuit crust than a light sponge topping.

You will need to marinate the fruit the day before. You may bake this dessert in a pie dish or six ovenproof bowls.

INGREDIENTS — SERVES 6

1 litre	(34 fl oz)	water
150g	(5½ oz)	sugar
100ml	(3½ fl oz)	dark rum
		zest of 1 orange
		juice of 1 orange
4		cloves
1		cinnamon stick
600g	(1¼ lb)	mixed dried fruit, roughly chopped
		icing sugar for dusting
		whipped cream

SPONGE

4		egg yolks
110g	(3¾ oz)	icing sugar
4		egg whites
1 tsp		ground cinnamon
85g	(3 oz)	plain flour

METHOD: At least 24 hours ahead of time, mix the water, sugar, rum, orange zest and juice, cloves and cinnamon together in a pot then briefly bring them to the boil. Place the dried fruit in a large bowl and, while the marinade is hot, pour it over. Cover and place in the refrigerator overnight.

Remove the cinnamon stick and the cloves from the marinated fruit then remove the fruit from the marinade and drain off the excess liquid. Place the fruit in a pie dish or six ovenproof bowls then lightly flatten the top. Pour some of the marinade over the fruit until it is barely covered. Put aside until required.

SPONGE: Place the egg yolks in a clean round-bottomed bowl. Add approximately one-third of the icing sugar then, using a fine whisk, beat until thick enough to leave a trail when the whisk is lifted.

In a separate bowl, whisk the egg whites until they are stiff, then gradually whisk in the remaining icing sugar until the mixture is stiff and glossy. Fold a little of the egg white into the egg yolk mixture.

Add the cinnamon to the flour. Carefully fold half the flour into the egg yolk, then fold in half the remaining egg white. Repeat with the remaining flour, finishing by carefully folding in the remaining whites.

TO COOK AND SERVE: Working quickly, evenly cover the fruit with the sponge mixture then place in a preheated 190°C (375°F) oven for 10–15 minutes with the fan on. It is important to get the dish in the oven immediately or the sponge will lose all the air.

Once the sponge is nicely browned on top, remove from the oven. Dust with icing sugar then serve with whipped cream.

LEMON AND PRALINE SYLLABUB
WITH NOUGATINE SHAPES

This is our variation of an old English dessert, and it may be served at lunch or dinner. It is simple to prepare, yet the subtle flavours of the lemon and cream combine so well with the nutty crunch of the praline.

Once you have prepared and ground the praline, any leftovers can be kept in an airtight container for later use. You can use praline for coating poached pears, or in ice cream, even just sprinkling around the dessert plate for effect.

PRALINE AND NOUGATINE: Roast the almonds in a preheated 230°C (450°F) oven for 3–5 minutes, until golden. Be careful as they brown quickly towards the end.

Mix the sugar, glucose and water together in a heavy-bottomed pot. Place over a steady heat and boil until the liquid is a light golden colour. Remove from the heat then carefully stir in the almonds.

Pour the mixture onto an oiled baking tray or non-stick teflon sheet. Spread out a little. Allow to completely cool and harden. Break the nougatine into pieces then grind to a fine praline powder in the blender. Reserve approximately 4 tsp of powder for the syllabub.

Sprinkle the remaining powder on a well-oiled baking tray or non-stick teflon sheet to approximately 6mm (¼") deep. Place in a preheated 230°C (450°F) oven and melt until it reaches a brown colour. Allow to cool slightly then, using a shaped cutter, sharp knife or pizza wheel, cut out triangles, hearts, etc. Make one or two shapes per syllabub. Place the nougatine shapes on greaseproof paper and allow to harden. Keep in an airtight container if they are not required right away.

SYLLABUB: Dissolve the sugar in the wine. In a stainless-steel bowl whisk the cream to a light to medium thickness. Add the lemon juice to the sugar and wine then pour into the cream, mixing slowly as you go. Allow the cream to thicken, but be careful not to over beat. Carefully mix in the reserved powdered praline.

Pour into long-stemmed wine or martini glasses. Cover with plastic wrap and place in the refrigerator for 2 hours before serving.

TO SERVE: Sprinkle a few chopped almonds over the syllabub then place the nougatine shapes on top, sticking up. Serve immediately.

INGREDIENTS — SERVES 6-8

PRALINE AND NOUGATINE

75g	(2½ oz)	flaked or fancy sliced almonds
350g	(12½ oz)	castor sugar
2 tbsp		liquid glucose (available from a pharmacy)
100ml	(3½ fl oz)	water

SYLLABUB

100g	(3½ oz)	castor sugar
60ml	(2 fl oz)	sweet white wine
600ml	(20 fl oz)	cream
		juice of 3-4 lemons
		chopped almonds to garnish

WHOLE ROAST PEARS WITH ICE CREAM AND CHOCOLATE SAUCE

Warm roasted pears with rich chocolate sauce are already a wonderful combination. Add to this homemade ice cream and the crunch of small sponge biscuits and you have a very tasty dessert.

Be sure to use firm pears to make it easier to roast them to the right degree. Preserve the stalk during the roasting process by wrapping aluminium foil around it, otherwise it will turn into charcoal. Prepare the sponge biscuits and chocolate sauce the day before. Make sure the biscuits are kept in an airtight container. The chocolate sauce will go firm in the refrigerator, so you will have to carefully remelt it over a pot of simmering water. The ice cream may be prepared well in advance and frozen. As for the pears, they can be roasted no more than a few hours in advance. Rewarm them on a baking tray in the oven just before serving.

INGREDIENTS — SERVES 6

SPONGE BISCUITS

3		egg yolks
60g	(2 oz)	castor sugar
2		egg whites
2¾ tbsp		cornflour
3½ tbsp		flour
		icing sugar for dusting

CHOCOLATE SAUCE

200g	(7 oz)	dark chocolate couverture
1¾ tbsp		castor sugar
175ml	(6 fl oz)	cream

ICE CREAM

1 litre	(34 fl oz)	vanilla ice cream (see page 132)

PEARS

6	firm pears icing sugar for dusting

SPONGE BISCUITS: Place the egg yolks in a round-bottomed bowl. Add one-third of the sugar then whisk until pale yellow. In a separate bowl whisk the egg whites until frothy, then slowly trickle in the remaining sugar, whisking as you go until the whites are stiff. Sift the cornflour then carefully fold into the egg whites. Incorporate the yolks into the egg whites, but do not over mix. Finally, sift the flour into the egg mixture and carefully fold in. The mixture must remain as firm as possible.

Line a baking tray with greaseproof paper or a non-stick teflon sheet. Using a piping bag with a size 1 plain nozzle, pipe 36–40 biscuits, 5.5cm x 2cm (2″ x ¾″). Lightly dust with icing sugar.

Bake in a preheated 190°C (375°F) oven for 8–10 minutes. While still warm place on a cake rack to cool, then store in an airtight container.

CHOCOLATE SAUCE: Finely chop the chocolate then melt in a bowl over a pot of simmering water. Add the sugar to the cream then heat to just below boiling point. Pour the cream into the chocolate, mixing as you pour. Once well mixed in, pass through a fine sieve into a clean bowl. Cover and put aside.

ICE CREAM: Prepare and store the vanilla ice cream as explained on page 132.

PEARS: Peel the pears then, using a medium-sized melon baller, remove all the seeds, working from the base of the pear. Be careful not to hollow the pear out more than is necessary.

Very liberally douse the pears in icing sugar. Space them well apart on a fine cake rack and place the rack over a roasting tin with a little water in it. Make sure the pears are well clear of the water, which will prevent excess icing sugar from burning as it runs off the pears during cooking.

Place the pears in a preheated 200°C (400°F) oven and cook with the fan on until the pears are just soft and brown. Check first after 15 minutes, then every 5 minutes. If the pears are becoming soft but not browning, increase the oven temperature. It may be necessary to lightly dust the pears with icing sugar and top up the water in the tray halfway through the cooking time. Do not allow the pears to become too soft — they will continue to cook for some time once removed from the oven.

Cool the pears slightly on the rack then carefully transfer to a baking tray ready for reheating. Do not refrigerate.

TO SERVE: Warm the chocolate sauce and reheat the pears. Place a warm pear on each warm plate. Pour some sauce around the pears and arrange three sponge biscuits and a ball of ice cream around each pear. Serve immediately.

CRÈME DE CASSIS MOUSSE
WITH RED BERRY COMPÔTE AND SABLÉ LEAVES

Crème de cassis is a liqueur made from blackcurrants. It is produced in many countries, but the French are thought to produce the best.

The red berries you use for the compôte depends on what is available, and summer is always the best time to find a good variety of red berries.

We use 50ml (1¾ fl oz) moulds for this dessert, but you may set the mousse in any dish.

The compôte will need to be prepared the day before, and the mousse may also be prepared a day in advance.

INGREDIENTS — SERVES 6-8

250ml	(8½ fl oz)	milk
4		egg yolks
60g	(2 oz)	castor sugar
60ml	(2 fl oz)	crème de cassis
3-4		gelatine leaves
150ml	(5 fl oz)	cream
		pâte sablée
		(see page 137)
		mint to garnish

COMPÔTE

600g	(1¼ lb)	mixed red berries (strawberries, raspberries, blackberries, blueberries)
100g	(3½ oz)	mixed red berries for marinating liquid
150ml	(5 fl oz)	port
3½ tbsp		red wine
		zest of ½ orange
½		cinnamon stick
100ml	(3½ fl oz)	sugar syrup (see page 134)

METHOD: Place the milk in a heavy-bottomed pot and bring to the boil. Whisk the egg yolks, sugar and crème de cassis to ribbon stage.

Pour on one-third of the boiling milk then mix together. Lower the heat then pour the egg mixture back into the remaining milk.

Stirring constantly with a wooden spoon, cook the custard until it coats the back of the spoon. Do not boil. Remove from the heat.

Soften the gelatine leaves in cold water then squeeze dry. Add to the hot custard and stir until dissolved. Pass through a fine sieve into a stainless-steel bowl.

Whip the cream lightly.

Place the custard over a bowl of ice and stir until it begins to thicken. Mix in the whipped cream.

Pour into six to eight 50ml (1¾ fl oz) moulds. Place in the refrigerator and allow to set for at least 3 hours.

COMPÔTE: Wash, hull and sort the berries. Place them in a medium-sized bowl. Place the remaining ingredients in a pot and bring to the boil. Simmer for 1 minute.

Pass through a fine sieve onto the prepared berries while still warm. Push through as much of the berry pulp as possible. Cover the compôte and place in the refrigerator overnight.

SABLÉ LEAVES: Roll out the sablé pastry to 3mm (⅛″) thick on a flat, well-floured surface.

Cut out three leaves for each portion, to your own pattern. Place them all on a baking tray and cook in a preheated 200°C (400°F) oven for 5-6 minutes. Remove from the oven and cool on a cake rack.

TO SERVE: Unmould the mousses by dipping them briefly into hot water then shake them out into flat soup plates.

Divide the compôte evenly between each portion around the crème de cassis mousse, serving the marinating liquid also.

Arrange the sablé leaves tidily on each one and serve at room temperature.

CARAMEL ICE CREAM OVER DARK AND WHITE CHOCOLATE SAUCES

The ingredients for this ice cream are almost the same as in the standard vanilla ice cream recipe, but they are prepared in a different way. The sugar is caramelised then cream is added to make a caramel sauce that flavours the ice cream.

You will need to prepare the ice cream a day in advance. The chocolate sauces may also be made in advance. Once chilled they will set, but may be warmed over a pot of simmering water then kept at room temperature ready for use.

INGREDIENTS — SERVES 6

12	slices or balls of caramel ice cream (see page 132)
150g (5½ oz)	bitter chocolate
200g (7 oz)	white chocolate
250ml (8½ fl oz)	milk
60ml (2 fl oz)	cream

METHOD: Prepare and store the ice cream according to the instructions on page 132. Make sure the storage container is well chilled before placing the ice cream in it. I would suggest putting it in the freezer for at least 1 hour first.

Melt the chocolate separately in two double saucepans or bains-marie. Bring the milk to the boil then add the cream. Pour half the milk and cream into each pot of chocolate, stirring as you pour. Continue to stir until each sauce is well combined.

Remove from the heat and pass each sauce through a fine sieve into a clean bowl. Cover with plastic wrap and allow to cool to room temperature.

TO SERVE: Place a baking tray in the freezer for 30 minutes. If slicing the ice cream, briefly dip the container in hot water then turn the ice cream out onto a cutting surface. Cut slices and place each on the chilled tray, then return to the freezer. Wrap any remaining ice cream in aluminium foil and store frozen.

Divide the chocolate sauces evenly between each plate, then place two slices or balls of ice cream on each. Serve immediately.

MULLED WINE BERRIES TOPPED WITH PORT AND ORANGE GRANITÉ

The choice of the berries you use in this simply prepared dessert is entirely up to you. Beautiful sun ripened raspberries, strawberries, kerriberries or blackberries, and blueberries are among the best combinations.

Prepare the mulled wine and marinate the berries, and prepare and freeze the granité, the day before. Once frozen the granité should resemble crushed ice, although because of the alcohol in the port it may be slightly slushy.

Serve in well chilled, long-stemmed glasses at lunch or on a warm summer's evening.

METHOD: Wash all the berries carefully then place in a medium-sized bowl.

MULLED WINE: Place all the mulled wine ingredients in a pot and bring to the boil. Skim off any impurities as they rise to the surface. Lower the heat and gently simmer for 2–3 minutes. Remove from the heat then allow to stand for 10 minutes. While still warm pour over the berries. Cover then place in the refrigerator overnight.

GRANITÉ: Quickly bring all the ingredients to the boil in a medium-sized pot. Pour into a flat dish or tray. Cool slightly then place in the freezer. Allow to freeze.

TO SERVE: Place six elegant glasses in the refrigerator to chill. Remove the berries from the mulled wine marinade and evenly divide them between each glass. Pour over the mulled wine until it barely covers the fruit. Keep the glasses of fruit in the refrigerator until you are ready to serve.

Scrape the granité off the tray, crushing with a heavy whisk if necessary. Spoon onto the berries and top with candied orange zest and a sprig of mint then serve immediately.

INGREDIENTS — SERVES 6

600–700g (1¼–1¾ lb)	mixed berries
	mint to garnish
	candied zest to garnish

MULLED WINE

100g (3½ oz)	red berries
250ml (8½ fl oz)	red wine
200ml (7 fl oz)	port
100g (3½ oz)	castor sugar
1	cinnamon stick
	zest of 1 orange
	zest of 1 lemon
	juice of 2 oranges
2	cloves

GRANITÉ

75g (2½ oz)	castor sugar
100ml (3½ fl oz)	orange juice
300ml (10 fl oz)	good port

FIG AND APPLE COMPÔTE
WITH FRANGELICO SAUCE AND WALNUT STICKS

Figs are a native of southwestern Asia and have been cultivated since ancient times. They thrive all around the Mediterranean basin and can be found in North and South America, parts of Africa and even Australia. Turkey, Greece and Portugal are important fig producing and exporting countries. Depending on the variety, figs range from a light green to purple, but all, when ripe, should be soft and moist inside with red centres.

The apple tree originally came from an area between the Black and Caspian Seas, but it is now grown in temperate climates worldwide. There are thousands of different varieties of apple, falling into three groups: eating apples, cooking apples and all-purpose apples that are good for both eating and cooking.

For this dessert we use Granny Smith or Royal Gala apples. Braeburn are also a good choice, but any all-purpose apple will do.

You will need to marinate the fruit overnight.

INGREDIENTS — SERVES 6–8

10–12		fresh figs
200ml	(7 fl oz)	orange juice
150ml	(5 fl oz)	lemon juice
200ml	(7 fl oz)	water
150g	(5½ oz)	castor sugar
		zest of 1 orange
1		cinnamon stick
3		cloves
4–5		apples
50g	(1½ oz)	sultanas

FRANGELICO SAUCE

6		egg yolks
100g	(3½ oz)	castor sugar
60ml	(2 fl oz)	frangelico
450ml	(15 fl oz)	milk

WALNUT STICKS

150g	(5½oz)	shelled walnuts
2		pieces of 2–3mm (1/12–1/8″) thick puff pastry, 20cm x 10cm (8″ x 4″)
1		beaten egg for egg wash
		icing sugar for dusting

METHOD: Carefully peel the figs, retaining their shape.

Place the orange and lemon juice, water, sugar, zest, cinnamon and cloves in a small pot. Bring to the boil then briefly plunge in the figs, four at a time. Place the figs on a tray to completely cool. Remove the liquid from the heat and keep aside.

Peel and quarter the apples. Remove the seeds then slice into thick wedges. Place the apple with a little water in a large non-reactive pot. Cover with a lid and cook over a gentle heat until soft. Stir regularly but try not to break the apple up. Add the sultanas and cook for 1 minute. Remove from the heat and place in a stainless-steel or plastic tray or bowl.

Cut the figs into halves if small or quarters if larger, then carefully mix with the apple. Pour over the fig poaching liquid, cover with plastic wrap and place in the refrigerator overnight.

FRANGELICO SAUCE: Place the yolks in a bowl then add the sugar and frangelico. Whisk well until at ribbon stage, when the whisk leaves tracks in the mixture. Put the milk in a heavy-bottomed pot and bring to the boil. Pour the milk into the egg mixture, whisking as you pour. Pour the custard back into the pot. Set over a low heat and cook, stirring constantly with a wooden spoon, until the custard coats the back of the spoon. Do not allow the custard to boil. Pass through a fine sieve into a clean bowl and cool completely, stirring from time to time.

Cover with plastic wrap and store in the refrigerator until required.

WALNUT STICKS: Place the walnuts in a food processor and blend until quite fine. Brush one piece of the puff pastry with egg wash then form three lines of ground walnut the length of the pastry.

Brush one side of the remaining piece of pastry with egg wash then lay over the pastry with the lines of walnut. Press together, making sure the pastry is formed around the lines of ground nut.

Place in the refrigerator for 15 minutes then liberally dust with icing sugar. Cut into twenty 1 cm (just under ½″) sticks, cutting across the pastry. Place the sticks on a baking tray, lined with a non-stick teflon sheet if possible, and bake until golden brown in a preheated 200°C (400°F) oven.

Cool on cake racks and store in an airtight container.

TO SERVE: Remove the cinnamon stick and cloves from the compôte. Drain off all the liquid. Form six to eight portions by pressing into a 7cm (2¾ ″) plain cutter. Press down firmly. Remove the cutter. Using a fish slice, place each portion on a flat plate. Spoon the sauce around the compôte then arrange three walnut sticks on each and serve.

MERINGUE NESTS WITH CHESTNUT CREAM, VANILLA ICE CREAM AND PLUM PURÉE

In this dessert we use a good quality commercial chestnut purée (purée de marrons) and imported French preserved chestnuts, which are available at any good delicatessen.

INGREDIENTS — SERVES 6-8

2	large egg whites
50g (1½ oz)	castor sugar
50g (1½ oz)	icing sugar
	vanilla ice cream
	(see page 132)
6-8	plums to garnish
	mint to garnish
6-8	preserved chestnuts
	to garnish

PLUM PURÉE

300g (10½ oz)	fresh red plums or
	bottled plums
150ml (5 fl oz)	sugar syrup
	(see page 134)

CHESTNUT CREAM

200g (7 oz)	chestnut purée
3½ tbsp	sugar syrup
100ml (3½ fl oz)	cream

METHOD: In a clean bowl, whisk the egg whites to a soft peak. Gradually whisk in the castor sugar a little at a time and beat steadily for 5 minutes. Sift the icing sugar then carefully fold into the meringue. Do not over mix.

Mark out six to eight 6cm (2¼″) diameter circles on a sheet of greaseproof paper.

Fit a nozzle with a 7mm (¼″) hole to a piping bag. Fill with the meringue mixture then, starting from the middle, pipe out the nests in a continuous coil with two additional coils on the outside edge to form the sides.

Place in a preheated 80°C (180°F) oven, with the fan on, for 2 hours to dry out and go crispy. Keep a close eye on the nests as they must not go brown. Open the oven door if they start to colour.

Cool on racks then store in an airtight container.

PLUM PURÉE: Place the plums and sugar syrup in a food processor and purée until smooth. Pass through a fine sieve into a clean bowl. Cover and store refrigerated until required.

CHESTNUT CREAM: Break the chestnut purée down with the sugar syrup into a smooth paste. Beat the cream until it is quite stiff then mix into the chestnut purée. The mixture should be of piping consistency.

TO SERVE: Place a small pool of plum purée on each plate. Evenly fill each nest with chestnut cream to just above the top then place on the plum purée. Arrange three small plum wedges on the side of each plate. Place a ball of vanilla ice cream in each nest then top with a preserved chestnut. Garnish with mint and serve immediately.

BREAD AND BUTTER PUDDING

From very humble beginnings, the bread and butter pudding has been elevated to stardom in recent years. Top restaurants have it on their menus and famous chefs such as Anton Mosimann have given bread and butter pudding international appeal. Even with all this attention it still remains very much as it originally was; such simplicity is difficult to improve on.

We like to serve this pudding with an accompaniment of stewed fruits, the variety depending on the season.

METHOD: Bring the milk, cream and vanilla pod to the boil in a large pot. Add the salt.

Beat the eggs and castor sugar together. Pour the hot milk and cream onto the eggs, stirring thoroughly as you pour. Pass through a fine sieve into a clean bowl.

Remove the crusts from the buttered bread. Drain the sultanas then sprinkle a few on the bottom of a 5cm (2″) deep pie dish or an ovenproof dish with a capacity of about 1 litre (34 fl oz). Arrange the bread evenly in the dish. Pour on some of the custard to soak the bread, preventing it from floating, then sprinkle over the rest of the sultanas. Pour in the remaining custard.

Place the pudding in a roasting tin then fill the tray with hot water to three-quarters of the way up the side of the dish. Place in a preheated 160°C (310°F) oven for 1 hour, with the fan on.

Bring the apricot jam to the boil with the water, stirring often, until the jam is melted. Continue to boil for 1 minute. Keep warm.

TO SERVE: Spread the warm jam over the pudding then allow to stand for 10 minutes at room temperature. Serve with stewed fruit.

INGREDIENTS — SERVES 6

300ml	(10 fl oz)	milk
300ml	(10 fl oz)	cream
½		vanilla pod, split
		pinch of salt
5		eggs
200g	(7 oz)	castor sugar
6		slices of white bread, well buttered
50g	(1½ oz)	sultanas, soaked in water until soft
100g	(3½ oz)	apricot jam
3½ tbsp		water
		icing sugar for dusting

CHOCOLATE AND RICE PUDDING

This dessert involves a certain amount of work, mainly because of the number of components. However, the final result is well worth the effort.

Use short grain rice that will become soft and mushy once cooked. A good quality dark chocolate will also give better results. We use a 6.5cm (2½") plain cutter to form the individual portions. If you don't have enough cutters the correct size, then a 15–20cm (6–8") flan ring may be used. The dessert is set up using the same method but served as a wedge cut with a hot sharp knife.

INGREDIENTS — SERVES 6-8

400ml	(13½ fl oz)	milk
450ml	(15 fl oz)	cream
½		vanilla pod, split
115g	(4 oz)	short grain rice
1¾ tbsp		castor sugar
115g	(4 oz)	dark chocolate
1½ tbsp		cocoa
30g	(1 oz)	unsalted butter
120ml	(4 fl oz)	cream
1		large egg yolk
25g	(1 oz)	pistachio nuts, chopped

ORANGE SAUCE

		zest of 2 oranges
75g	(2½ oz)	castor sugar
450ml	(15 fl oz)	orange juice
1 tsp		arrowroot
		pulp of 3 passionfruit

GARNISH

30-40	orange segments
30-40	chocolate sablé leaves (see page 137)
6	small quenelles of orange ice cream (see page 132)
6	sugar cages (optional) (see page 134)
6	sprigs of mint

METHOD: Put the milk, cream and vanilla in a medium-sized heavy-bottomed pot. Bring to the boil then add the rice and gently simmer for 25 minutes or until the rice is soft. Stir the rice regularly with a wooden spoon to prevent sticking.

Once cooked move the rice from the heat, remove the vanilla pod and stir in the sugar. Allow to cool. The rice mixture should be quite thick. If it is not, continue to reduce it over a gentle heat.

Place six 6.5cm (2½") cutters or one small flan ring on a flat tray. Three-quarters fill each cutter or the ring with rice pudding, pushing the rice down with a spoon to expel the air. Refrigerate for at least 20 minutes.

Finely chop the chocolate then place in a round-bottomed bowl over a pot of simmering water. Completely melt all the chocolate.

Add the cocoa to the butter then beat together until the butter is soft. Add to the melted chocolate and roughly mix in. Whisk the cream into the chocolate. Remove the chocolate from the heat then whisk in the egg yolks one at a time. Finally stir in the chopped pistachios. Cover the chocolate and place on the bench to cool and set to a paste. Once thick, spoon onto the rice and smooth the top. Refrigerate to set the chocolate.

ORANGE SAUCE: Place the orange zest in a pot and just cover with water. Add a teaspoon of the castor sugar then cook the zest until tender. Add the orange juice and the rest of the sugar then bring to the boil. Dilute the arrowroot in a little water then whisk into the boiling orange juice. Simmer for 30 seconds. Pass through a fine sieve into a clean bowl and add the passionfruit pulp and the cooked zest. Mix together then cover and place in the refrigerator until required.

TO SERVE: Carefully place the rice and chocolate-filled cutters in the centre of six cold plates by sliding a fish slice or palette knife under them and easing off the tray. Wrap a hot cloth around each one to release the cutter from the pudding. If using a flan ring, remove the ring with a hot teatowel, then cut into wedges and place on each plate.

Evenly spoon the orange sauce around each portion and arrange the orange segments and sablé leaves on each plate. Top with a small quenelle of orange ice cream and a sprig of mint, then place the sugar cage on top.

Serve immediately.

FRUIT FLAN

At Christmas and New Year, or at special buffets, we serve a trolley or table of all our favourite pies, tartes, flans, gâteaux and desserts. They all look and taste beautiful, but the one that stands out is the most traditional, the fruit flan.

The bright shining colours of the fruit, perfectly arranged over the beautifully smooth and delicate crème pâtissière held in my favourite sweet pastry, rich, golden sablé, ensure this is a favourite with our guests.

The variety of fruit and pattern is up to you and may depend on seasonal availability. You will need a 28cm (11") fluted flan case.

INGREDIENTS — MAKES 1

500g (18 oz)	pâte sablée (see page 137)
1	beaten egg for egg wash

CRÈME PÂTISSIÈRE

550ml (18½ fl oz)	milk
1	vanilla pod, split
6	egg yolks
125g (4½ oz)	castor sugar
60g (2 oz)	flour

FRUIT GARNISH

30–35	blackberries or kerriberries
5–6	oranges
3	grape halves with seeds removed
1	kiwifruit, thinly sliced
15	strawberries

APRICOT GLAZE

300g (10½ oz)	apricot jam
60–80 ml (2–3 fl oz)	water

METHOD: Roll out the pâte sablée until it is 2cm (¾") larger in diameter than the flan case. Do not over handle as the pastry will become difficult to work with. Use the pastry while it is still firm but not hard.

Lay the pastry over the flan case by loosely rolling it around the rolling pin then unrolling it over the case. Press the pastry into shape with your fingers without stretching it. Cut off the excess pastry by firmly rolling the pin across the top of the case. Using a fork, make several holes in the base.

Line the case with greaseproof paper then fill with beans or rice. Bake in a preheated 200 °C (400 °F) oven until the rim of the flan case is light brown.

Remove the paper and beans or rice and return the case to the oven and continue to bake until well browned. Cool slightly then liberally brush the inside with beaten egg. Return to the oven and continue to bake for 1 minute. Allow to completely cool.

CRÈME PÂTISSIÈRE: Bring the milk to the boil with the vanilla pod.

In a large bowl beat the egg yolks and sugar together until pale. Sieve in the flour and mix together well.

Remove the vanilla from the milk then gradually add to the egg mixture, stirring constantly as you pour. Return the mixture to a gentle heat in a clean pot and bring slowly back to the boil, stirring constantly. Cook for 2–3 minutes over a very gentle heat. Allow the crème pâtissère to cool a little, but while it is still warm and just runny pour into the baked flan case. Evenly spread over the case. Cool, allowing the crème to set.

FRUIT GARNISH: Skin, peel and slice your fruit selection, then arrange over the crème pâtissière. Use a small vegetable knife to help position the fruit. Work from the middle to the outside.

APRICOT GLAZE: Place the apricot jam and water in a pot and slowly bring to the boil. Pass through a fine sieve into a clean bowl. While the glaze is still hot, dab it carefully over the fruit with a brush. Cover the fruit completely.

TO SERVE: Allow the flan to cool completely then serve on a silver tray, or cover in plastic wrap and store in the refrigerator until needed.

APPLE FRITTERS WITH CALVADOS SORBET

These apple fritters are so easy to make, yet so tasty. Any good apple is suitable, although we find the sharper-flavoured varieties such as Granny Smith best. If calvados is not available, use apple concentrate mixed with a little brandy.

INGREDIENTS — SERVES 6

SORBET

100g	(3½ oz)	castor sugar
300ml	(10 fl oz)	water
		juice of 2 lemons
100ml	(3½ fl oz)	calvados

APPLE FRITTERS

		juice of 2 lemons
1 litre	(34 fl oz)	water
3–4		apples
1		egg
100g	(3½ oz)	castor sugar
1½ tsp		ground cinnamon
250ml	(8½ fl oz)	milk
125g	(4½ oz)	flour
		vegetable oil for frying
		flour for coating

SORBET: Mix all the ingredients together making sure to dissolve the sugar. Freeze to piping consistency, whisking vigorously at regular intervals to achieve a smooth texture. Alternatively, freeze in a sorbet machine. Store in the freezer.

APPLE FRITTERS: Add the lemon juice to the water. Core the apples, leaving them whole, then peel. Slice into 12 rings 1cm (½″) thick. Keep the rings in the lemon water to prevent discolouring.

Beat the egg then mix in a teaspoon of the sugar and half a teaspoon of the cinnamon. Add the milk. Sprinkle on the flour, mixing vigorously, until a coating consistency is achieved. Pass the batter through a fine sieve into a clean bowl and allow to stand for 15 minutes at room temperature.

Heat a large pot of vegetable oil or a friture for deep frying to approximately 180°C (350°F). Pat the apple rings dry then coat in flour. Shake off any excess flour then dip into the batter. Shake off excess batter then drop into the oil. Cook on both sides until golden brown. Handle the fritters carefully to avoid making holes in the batter. Drain on kitchen paper then toss in a mixture of the rest of the castor sugar and the cinnamon.

TO SERVE: Put two warm fritters on each plate. Place a scoop of calvados sorbet on each and serve immediately.

CHERRIES WITH SNOW EGGS

Only in the summer months are fresh cherries widely available, although some bottled and tinned fruit can be just as good.

Cherries originated from and were first cultivated in Assyria. The Romans brought the cherry back to Italy in 74 BC and within 200 years cherry trees were thriving throughout Great Britain and northern Europe.

Snow eggs are often served over a pond of crème anglaise. They are very light and cook quickly. They may be prepared in advance and stored, covered, on wet greaseproof paper in the refrigerator.

METHOD: Stone the cherries then place half in a food processor or liquidiser and purée until smooth. Pass through a fine sieve into a clean bowl, pushing through as much of the purée as possible. Mix in the sugar, juice and kirsch. Cover then place in the refrigerator.

Cut the remaining cherries in half then place in a bowl ready for use.

SNOW EGGS: In a large clean bowl or electric mixer, beat the egg whites to a stiff snow, adding the pinch of salt then the sugar in a thin stream as you whisk.

Bring a shallow pan of water to the boil then lower the heat to just below boiling.

Using two serving spoons, shape the meringue into oval shapes then place in the just simmering water. You will require two small or one large snow egg per portion.

Cook each snow egg for 45 seconds on one side then carefully turn and cook for a further 45 seconds. Larger snow eggs will need 1 minute each side.

Remove from the water with a slotted spoon and place on damp greaseproof paper. Cover and store in the refrigerator.

TO SERVE: Evenly pour the prepared cherry purée into rimmed bowls or plates. Divide the cherries evenly between each portion then place the snow eggs on top. Garnish with mint and serve.

Vanilla sponge fingers (see page 64) make a good accompaniment as well.

INGREDIENTS — SERVES 6

1.4kg (3 lb)	cherries
2½ tbsp	icing sugar
	juice of 1 lemon
	juice of 1 orange
60ml (2 fl oz)	kirsch
	mint to garnish

SNOW EGGS

4	egg whites
	pinch of salt
150g (5½ oz)	castor sugar

CHOCOLATE TERRINE
WITH ROAST PEARS AND A NUT CRUST

This is a great dessert that can be made a day or two in advance. Use good quality chocolate and make sure the pears are firm. Winter Coles are good, but any unblemished firm pear will do. We usually serve a red berry coulis, as it helps balance the richness of the chocolate.

INGREDIENTS — SERVES 8–10

2		medium-sized pears
		icing sugar for dusting pears
50g	(1½ oz)	shelled walnuts
50g	(1½ oz)	shelled hazelnuts
125g	(4½ oz)	castor sugar
3		egg yolks
85g	(3 oz)	cocoa
150g	(5½ oz)	soft unsalted butter
75g	(2½ oz)	dark chocolate
2½ tbsp		icing sugar
250ml	(8½ fl oz)	cream
		fruit to garnish
		mint to garnish

COULIS

150g	(5½ oz)	fresh or bottled berries (raspberries, blackberries, boysenberries, strawberries)
300ml	(10 fl oz)	sugar syrup (see page 134)

METHOD: Peel the pears then cut in half. Using a melon baller, remove the seeds. Make sure the pears are very dry then liberally coat in icing sugar on both sides. Put a little water in a roasting tin and place the pears on a cake rack in the tin. Bake in a preheated 220°C (425°F) oven for 15–20 minutes, until the pears turn brown and are soft. It may be necessary to top up the water in the tin.

Allow to completely cool on the rack.

Roast the nuts in the oven until light brown. Remove the husks from the hazelnuts by rolling together in a brown paper bag, then grind all the nuts to medium-fine.

Brush a 7.5cm x 21cm (3″ x 8″) loaf tin or mould with butter, coating well. Place the ground nuts in the mould then roll around until all sides are evenly coated. Tip out and keep any excess nuts then place in the refrigerator to firm up.

Add the castor sugar to the egg yolks then beat together until the mixture is pale.

In a separate bowl add the cocoa to the soft butter and beat together well.

Melt the chocolate over a pot of simmering water than add it to the egg yolks, mixing as you go. Thoroughly beat together.

Add the chocolate mixture to the butter mixture, and combine.

Add the icing sugar to the cream then lightly beat. Add the cream to the chocolate and beat until smooth.

Using a piping bag, half fill the mould with chocolate mixture, making sure there are no air pockets. Place the cold pears on top, scooped-out side up, then press down slightly. Fill the mould with remaining chocolate and tap lightly to remove any air. Sprinkle the excess nuts over the top and place in the refrigerator to harden for approximately 3 hours.

COULIS: Purée the berries and syrup together then pass through a fine sieve into a clean bowl.

TO SERVE: Quickly dip the mould in hot water then turn out onto a cutting board. Using a warm knife, evenly slice the terrine.

Place a pool of the coulis in the middle of a clean plate then spread a little. Put a slice of the terrine onto the coulis. Dust the edge of the plate with icing sugar then garnish with a little fruit and a sprig of mint and serve.

MIXED NUT FLAN

The filling for this flan is prepared in a similar way to our Mixed Nut Pithivier (**Huka Lodge's Cook Book**). However, as the filling is exposed to the heat during the cooking process a beautiful crunchy crust is achieved.

We accompany the flan with a fresh fruit purée. The choice fruit for the purée is entirely up to you but we find apricot purée a successful accompaniment. The flan case is not baked blind in advance because the nut filling takes some time to cook.

This moist flan may be eaten warm or cold. The recipe makes one whole flan in a flan dish with a removable base. It will keep for some time in a biscuit tin.

INGREDIENTS — SERVES 8-12

PASTRY

200g	(7 oz)	unsalted butter
100g	(3½ oz)	icing sugar
2-3		egg yolks
250g	(9 oz)	flour
		pinch of salt

FILLING

110g	(4 oz)	shelled hazelnuts
110g	(4 oz)	shelled walnuts
110g	(4 oz)	shelled almonds
170g	(6 oz)	unsalted butter
350g	(12½ oz)	icing sugar
50g	(1½ oz)	flour
4		eggs

FRUIT PURÉE

150g	(5½ oz)	fresh fruit
100ml	(3½ fl oz)	sugar syrup
		(see page 134)

GARNISH

	icing sugar for dusting
	fresh fruit
	mint
	tuile baskets (optional) (see page 128)

PASTRY: Cream the butter and icing sugar together then beat in the yolks a little at a time until a smooth consistency is achieved.

Sieve the flour then add the salt. Using a wooden spoon gradually add the flour to the butter mixture. Do not over mix. Sprinkle some flour onto the bench and knead the pastry briefly. Cover then rest in the refrigerator until required.

FILLING: Place all the nuts in a food processor and blend until well ground. With a wooden spoon, beat the butter until soft then work in the ground nuts, icing sugar and flour. Add the eggs one at a time and mix in.

On a well floured flat surface, roll the pastry to a thickness of approximately 6mm (¼"). Carefully line a non-stick 29cm (11½") flan case with the pastry, making sure there are no holes. Pour in the prepared nut mix then place in a preheated 165°C (325°F) oven for 50-55 minutes, with the fan off.

FRUIT PURÉE: Purée the fruit with the sugar syrup until it is smooth. Pass through a fine sieve into a clean bowl.

TO SERVE: Once the flan is cooked remove from the oven and allow to cool a little or, if desired, allow to go cold. Dust the top of the flan with icing sugar then place under a very hot grill until the sugar caramelises.

Cut into wedges then place each on a plate. Spoon a puddle of the fruit purée next to the wedge. Garnish with fruit and a sprig of mint. Serve immediately.

We also accompany the mixed nut flan with tuile baskets (see page 128) filled with fresh berries and dusted with icing sugar.

MARINATED STRAWBERRY TERRINE
WITH LIME SYRUP

*This strawberry terrine is similar in construction to the fruit terrine in **Huka Lodge's Cook Book**. The flavour of the fruit and liquid that will become the jelly is concentrated through a simple marinating process.*

Use deep red and firm strawberries, with no blemishes, and dark green limes. You will need to marinate the strawberries the day before the dessert is required. You will need a 1.4 litre (3 US pint) Le Creuset or similar terrine mould. Once prepared this terrine will keep for several days well covered in the refrigerator.

METHOD: Slice the larger strawberries in half and place them all in a large stainless-steel bowl. Mix the cointreau, orange juice and sugar together then pour over the strawberries. Cover and place in the refrigerator overnight.

Next day drain the liquid from the fruit into a pot and warm over a medium heat. Soften the gelatine leaves in cold water, then completely dissolve them in the warm marinating liquid. Pass the liquid through a fine sieve into a clean bowl and allow to cool. Pour just enough of the jelly into the mould to cover the bottom. Allow to set in the refrigerator.

Once the jelly is set spread the strawberries evenly in the mould. Barely cover the strawberries with the cool marinating liquid, allow to set in the refrigerator, then top with the remaining liquid. This will prevent the fruit from floating. Place in the refrigerator for 1 hour before serving.

LIME SYRUP: Combine the lime and lemon juice and sugar in a pot. Bring to the boil, skimming off any impurities as they rise. Dilute the arrowroot in a little water then thicken the juice.

Just cover the zest with water and add a pinch of castor sugar. Cook over a steady heat until the zest is tender and all the liquid has evaporated.

Pass the syrup through a fine sieve onto the zest, pour into a clean bowl, cover and store in the refrigerator until required.

TO SERVE: Carefully release the jelly from the rim of the terrine. Place the terrine in warm water for a count of 10. Remove from the water, turn the terrine on its side and slide a flat knife or palette knife down the side to release the fruit terrine from the mould. Turn upside down and ease out onto a cutting surface. Mark out the cutting points and slice with a warm, sharp knife or electric knife.

Place the slices on chilled plates and spoon on the lime syrup. Garnish each plate with five lime segments per plate and mint. If possible allow to stand at room temperature for 10-15 minutes before serving.

INGREDIENTS — SERVES 10-12

850g (1 ¾ lb)	ripe strawberries, hulled and rinsed
200ml (7 fl oz)	cointreau
500ml (17 fl oz)	orange juice
50g (1 ½ oz)	castor sugar
7	gelatine leaves
7-8	limes to garnish
	mint to garnish

LIME SYRUP

250ml (8 ½ fl oz)	lime juice
3 ½ tbsp	lemon juice
75g (2 ½ oz)	castor sugar
1 tsp	arrowroot
	zest of 3 limes
	pinch of castor sugar

CARAMELISED PUMPKIN TERRINE WITH VANILLA ICE CREAM

In this wonderful dessert, smooth pumpkin purée combines with a light custard.

As the terrine has an egg custard base, take care during the cooking process not to damage the setting properties of the egg. The terrine must be cooked at a low temperature in a water bath. As it is baked in a deep mould the cooking time is long, but the result is well worth it.

We use a 7.5cm x 21cm (3" x 8") aluminium loaf tin, which is 6.5cm (2½") deep and has a liquid capacity of 800ml (27 fl oz). However, the pumpkin custard could be baked in smaller dariole moulds, and this would shorten the cooking time considerably.

Ginger ice cream is a nice alternative to vanilla ice cream in this dish. The terrine may be prepared the day before.

INGREDIENTS — SERVES 6-8

		vanilla ice cream
		(see page 132)
400g	(14 oz)	crown pumpkin, diced
		juice of 1 lemon
200ml	(7 fl oz)	milk
¼		vanilla pod, split
4		eggs
3		egg yolks
210g	(7½ fl oz)	castor sugar
200ml	(7 fl oz)	water

METHOD: Prepare and store vanilla ice cream according to instructions on page 132. Steam the pumpkin until it is very soft. Cool slightly then push through a fine sieve using the back of a ladle. Mix in the lemon juice then place in a bowl and cover. Keep at room temperature.

Pour the milk into a pot and add the vanilla. Bring to the boil. Beat the eggs, egg yolks and 100g (3½ oz) of the sugar together until pale yellow. Pour the hot milk into the egg mixture, stirring as you pour. Pass through a fine sieve into a clean bowl.

Mix one-third of the custard into the pumpkin purée and stir to a paste. Add the remaining custard, mixing well to ensure there are no lumps of pumpkin. Cover and put aside.

Place the rest of the sugar and the water in a heavy-bottomed pot. Cook over a steady heat until a rich, dark amber caramel is reached. Keep a close eye on the caramel as it must not become too dark and bitter. Stand by with a little water to halt the caramelising process if necessary. Be careful when adding water to hot caramel as there will be a violent reaction.

Allow the caramel to cool just slightly then pour over the base of the tin. Stir the pumpkin custard then pour into the tin over the toffee.

Place the pumpkin terrine on a teatowel in the bottom of a small roasting tin then pour in hot water until it reaches halfway up the side of the mould. Bake in a preheated 150°C (300°F) oven for 30 minutes then lower the heat to 100°C (210°F) and bake for 1½–1¾ hours more.

Remove the terrine from the water bath. The pumpkin terrine may seem 'wobbly' under the crust, but the heat trapped inside will set the terrine during the cooling time.

Cool at room temperature for 10–15 minutes then cover in plastic wrap and place in the refrigerator to completely chill, overnight if possible.

TO SERVE: Loosen the edges of the pumpkin terrine with your finger tips, then dip the mould in hot water for the count of 15. Run a small knife carefully around the edge of the custard, being careful to angle the blade against the metal.

Turn the mould upside down on a shallow tray so you do not lose the caramel sauce. Slowly ease the terrine out of its mould. If it won't come out, carefully poke a knife up the side to break the suction. Slice the terrine into portions by holding a fish slice against the end of the terrine, making your slice, then easing back with the portion attached to the fish slice. Transfer to a serving plate. Place on two quenelles of vanilla ice cream, spoon a little of the caramel liquid over the terrine and serve immediately.

SAVARINS WITH BANANA ICE CREAM AND SAUTÉED BANANAS

Today's savarin has evolved from the eastern European baba. Opinions vary about the origin of the baba: some say it was part of the traditional Russian Easter feast, others that King Stanislaus I of Poland invented it in the eighteenth century and named it after Ali Baba. The baba was incorporated into French classic cuisine and refined, ending up as the savarin now known the world over.

You will need ten 6cm (2½") savarin moulds. You may prepare just one large one, but cooking and proving times will alter. The savarins, syrup and ice cream may be prepared well in advance.

INGREDIENTS — SERVES 10

1 litre	(34 fl oz)	banana ice cream (see page 132)
425g	(15 oz)	flour
1 tsp		salt
15g	(½ oz)	fresh yeast
100ml	(3½ fl oz)	warm milk
150g	(5½ oz)	unsalted butter
50g	(1½ oz)	castor sugar
4		eggs
		orange segments to garnish

RUM SYRUP

500ml	(17 fl oz)	water
225g	(8 oz)	castor sugar
1		cinnamon stick
25g	(1 oz)	fresh ginger, roughly chopped, or ½ tsp ground ginger
100ml	(3½ fl oz)	dark rum

SAUTÉED BANANAS AND SAUCE

50g	(1½ oz)	unsalted butter
75g	(2½ oz)	brown sugar
		zest of 1 orange
3½ tbsp		orange juice
3½ tbsp		white rum
6		small, firm bananas
		clarified butter to sauté

METHOD: Prepare and store the banana ice cream well in advance.

To make the savarins, sieve the flour and salt into a warm bowl. Dissolve the yeast in the warm milk. Make a well in the flour and pour in the milk and yeast. Sprinkle a little of the flour over the milk. Cover with a clean cloth and place in a warm place to ferment. Melt the butter then add the sugar and eggs. Lightly mix together.

When the yeast begins to break through the flour, add the egg mixture then knead to an elastic dough. Do not over knead as the dough must not be too firm. Prove the dough in a warm place, covered with a cloth, until it has doubled in size.

Brush all the savarin moulds with soft butter, then dust with flour. Shake off the excess flour. Place the dough in a piping bag with a wide, plain nozzle, and half fill each mould with dough. Cover the moulds and prove in a warm place until doubled in size.

Bake the savarins in a preheated 200°C (400°F) oven for 14–18 minutes. Cool a little, then place on a cake rack.

RUM SYRUP: Place all the syrup ingredients in a pot and bring to the boil. Remove from the heat and cool to lukewarm. Using a perforated spoon dunk the savarins in the rum syrup until they have absorbed as much as possible. Take care how you handle them as they break easily. Place the soaked savarins on a tray in the refrigerator to completely cool.

SAUTÉED BANANAS AND SAUCE: Melt the unsalted butter in a pan. Add the brown sugar, zest and juice. Cook for 2 minutes then add the rum. Allow the alcohol to flambé. If the sauce is not for immediate use, cover it and put it aside until required. Do not store in the refrigerator.

Using a large sauté pan, melt a little clarified butter over a high heat. Peel the bananas and cut in half lengthways. Very quickly brown the bananas on the round side, then place on a baking tray. Do this in two batches or more, wiping out the sauté pan between each batch. Do not let the bananas become mushy.

TO SERVE: Place a soaked savarin in the centre of each plate. Warm the bananas a little then divide them between the portions, placing them beside each savarin. Heat the sauce and spoon it on and around the bananas. Garnish with orange segments, then place a ball of banana ice cream on top of the savarin. Serve immediately.

PEAR MOUSSE
WITH GINGER AND COCOA SABAYON

Any variety of pear can be used in this dessert. The only requirement is that the pear is ripe and juicy, with a natural sweetness.

In the sabayon we use blanched fresh ginger root. A native of Southeast Asia, this root is readily available, but be sure the root is tight and firm.

You may set the pear mousse in 150ml (5 fl oz) moulds or pour it all into one serving dish.

The sabayon must be served immediately as it will not stay fluffy for too long. The mousse may be prepared the day before, if covered and kept in the refrigerator.

INGREDIENTS — SERVES 6

400g (14 oz)	peeled and cored fresh pears
450ml (15 fl oz)	water
450ml (15 fl oz)	dry white wine
200g (7 oz)	sugar
	juice of 1 lemon
3½–4	gelatine leaves
200ml (7 fl oz)	cream
1	egg white

SABAYON

50g (1½ oz)	finely chopped fresh ginger root
1 tsp	castor sugar
5	egg yolks
1 tsp	cocoa
100ml (3½ fl oz)	sugar syrup (see page 134)

GARNISH

6	pear hats made from the cooked stalk and top of a pear (optional)
	mint
18	tuiles (see page 128)
	mandarin or orange segments

METHOD: Cut the pears into quarters.

Mix the water, wine, sugar and juice together in a pot then add the pear. Do this quickly to prevent the pear from discolouring. Place over a medium heat and cook until the pear is soft right through. Remove the pear from the cooking liquid and allow to drain well.

Soak the gelatine leaves in cold water until soft then squeeze dry.

Place the cooked and drained pear in a food processor and purée until smooth. Transfer to a large stainless-steel bowl and add the soaked gelatine leaves while the purée is still hot. If necessary return to the heat, stirring constantly, until all the gelatine has dissolved. Pass the purée through a sieve into a clean bowl, pushing through as much as possible.

Lightly whip the cream and beat the egg white until fluffy.

Cool the pear purée over ice until it begins to thicken. Mix in the cream then carefully fold in the egg white.

Pour into six moulds or a serving dish and place in the refrigerator for 2 hours.

SABAYON: Place the finely chopped ginger in a small pot. Just cover with water. Add the sugar then cook over a gentle heat until all the water has evaporated.

Place the ginger in a sabayon basin or round-bottomed bowl. Add the egg yolks and cocoa, mix together with a whisk. Add the sugar syrup.

TO SERVE: Unmould the pear mousses by dipping very briefly in hot water, then shaking out onto a plate. Alternatively, evenly spoon the set mousse onto the plates.

Place the sabayon mixture over a pot of simmering water. Using a balloon whisk, beat the mixture until fluffy and at least doubled in quantity. Continue to whisk until the whisk leaves tracks.

Divide the sabayon evenly between each mousse then top with the pear hats. Garnish with mint, tuiles and mandarin or orange segments and serve immediately.

FRUIT CAKE

Traditionally this type of fruit cake has been reserved for festive occasions such as Christmas and weddings, but we find this uniced fruit cake ideal for morning and afternoon tea, with coffee after dinner or whenever friends come to call.

This cake will keep for several weeks if kept airtight in a cool place and, as with most cakes of this type, it tastes far better after a couple of days.

The cake will remain quite moist because of the high fruit content but will take some time to cook as the heat takes a long time to penetrate the mixture.
To prevent over colouring on the outside, wrap the tin in three or four layers of newspaper held in place with string. The heat in the oven is not sufficient to burn the paper, although it will brown. If the top of the cake begins to get too dark, cover with aluminium foil.

You can make up your own favourite fruit mixture to the quantity listed or buy ready mixed fruit, which will have a good variety of dried fruits and mixed peel.

INGREDIENTS — MAKES 1

1.2kg	(2½ lb)	mixed dried fruit
450ml	(15 fl oz)	ginger ale
1 tbsp		medium sherry
250g	(9 oz)	butter
250g	(9 oz)	castor sugar
1 tbsp		golden syrup
4		eggs
300g	(10½ oz)	flour
1 tsp		baking powder
1 tsp		mixed spice
1 tsp		ground cinnamon
100g	(3½ oz)	finely ground almonds
½ tsp		vanilla essence
		icing sugar for dusting

METHOD: Soak the fruit in the ginger ale and sherry overnight.

Cream the butter and sugar, then add the golden syrup and the eggs, one at a time, and mix well.

Sieve the flour, baking powder, mixed spice and cinnamon together then mix into the butter mixture.

Drain the excess liquid from the soaked fruit and add to the flour base, then mix in the ground almonds and vanilla essence. Mix all the ingredients together well.

Line a 20–23cm (8–9″) square cake tin with greaseproof paper on the inside and tie newspaper around the outside of the tin. Pour the cake mixture into the tin and carefully smooth the top.

Place the tin in a preheated 180°C (350°F) oven and bake for 20 minutes. Lower the temperature to 150°C (300°F) and continue to bake for 3½ hours or until a skewer poked into the centre of the cake comes out clean. Cover the top of the cake with aluminium foil if it begins to darken too much.

Remove from the oven and allow to stand in a cool place (not the refrigerator) for one day before removing from the tin.

TO SERVE: If serving the cake whole, just dust the top with icing sugar and cut as required with a sharp knife. Serve with anything from mulled wine to coffee.

SAUTÉED PINEAPPLE OVER CARAMEL SAUCE

Christopher Columbus first encountered the pineapple on his arrival in the Caribbean, but it is a native of South America. The pineapple grows on the ananas tree and is actually a tight cluster of small fruits that form one large fruit. It is available year round and is cultivated throughout the world's tropical regions. It is ready to eat when there are no green areas on the rind and the crest of leaves can be easily plucked.

CARAMEL SAUCE: Put the sugar and water in a heavy-bottomed pot and place over a high heat and cook until the liquid turns a deep amber. While the sugar is caramelising heat the cream in another pot to just below boiling point.

Remove the toffee from the heat then add the cream a little at a time. Be very careful as there will be a great deal of steam and possibly some splatters. If necessary return the sauce to a gentle heat to dissolve any lumps of toffee.

Pass through a fine sieve into a clean bowl, cover and keep at room temperature. If the caramel sauce is too thick once cooled, thin with sugar syrup or a little cream.

PINEAPPLE: Peel the pineapple by grasping it by the leaves and cutting through the rind with a long sharp knife, then, with the knife on a slight angle, carefully removing the rind by rotating the pineapple. Top and tail then remove any remaining rind with the point of a sharp knife. Slice the pineapple into even rings then, using a sharp plain cutter, stamp out the hard core.

Using a large sauté pan, melt a knob of clarified butter over a high heat. Sprinkle a little of the sugar over both sides of the pineapple rings then, in batches of three or four, sauté on both sides until they brown. Place the browned rings on a tray and keep warm.

TO SERVE: Warm the caramel sauce and divide evenly between each plate. Place two warm pineapple rings on the sauce. Garnish with the sugar runouts and serve while warm.

INGREDIENTS — SERVES 6

CARAMEL SAUCE

250g (9 oz)	castor sugar
150ml (5 fl oz)	water
250ml (8½ fl oz)	cream

PINEAPPLE

12	fresh pineapple rings
50g (1½ oz)	castor sugar
	clarified butter to sauté
6	sugar runouts (see page 134)

APRICOT CRÈME BRÛLÉE

This is a variation of the classical vanilla crème brûlée, that may be prepared using fresh apricots poached in advance or bottled fruit when fresh is out of season. The brûlée may be prepared up to 12 hours in advance.

INGREDIENTS — SERVES 6

½	vanilla pod, split
250ml (8½ fl oz)	cream
2 tbsp	brandy (optional)
8	egg yolks
4 tbsp	castor sugar
6	cooked apricot halves, roughly chopped
6	nice-shaped, even-sized apricot halves
	brown sugar
	mint for garnish

METHOD: Place the vanilla pod with the cream in a pot over a high heat and bring almost to the boil.

Meanwhile beat the egg yolks and sugar together until they have become light yellow and doubled in quantity. Pour on the scalded cream, mixing as you go. Remove the vanilla pod.

Place in a bain-marie and continue to cook, stirring constantly, until the custard coats the back of a wooden spoon. The custard must be quite thick. Add the brandy.

Put chopped apricot in the bottom of six standard ramekins then evenly pour the custard into each. Place in the refrigerator and allow to set. If you have not cooked the custard enough initially, the brûlée will not set.

TO SERVE: Place a nicely formed apricot half on each brûlée and press down very gently. Evenly sprinkle brown sugar over the exposed custard to about 3mm (⅛″) thick. Using a damp cloth, clean the sides and rim of each ramekin.

In batches of two or three, caramelise the sugar under a hot grill. Serve the crème brûlée while the sugar is still just warm. Garnish with a sprig of mint.

ORANGE AND CHAMPAGNE TIMBALE WITH MELON PURÉE

Although we have used orange segments in this recipe, any variety of citrus fruit will work. A combination of pink grapefruit, orange and lime can be very effective in both taste and presentation.

We use 150ml (5 fl oz) timbale moulds, but any one-portion mould will be all right.

Be sure to use non-reactive moulds when using acid ingredients, or if food is to be stored for some time in the mould.

The orange timbales may be prepared a day in advance, left in their moulds, covered and kept in the refrigerator.

METHOD: Top and tail all the oranges. Using a small sharp knife, cut around the contours of the fruit removing the skin and all the white pith. Working over a bowl to collect all the juices, remove each orange segment from the membrane with the knife. Place the segments on kitchen paper to drain. Cover and place in the refrigerator.

Squeeze any remaining juice from the orange frame once the segments have been removed. You will require 150ml (5 fl oz) of juice, so add extra juice if necessary.

Place the champagne, orange juice and sugar in a pot and heat. Soak the gelatine leaves in cold water until soft then squeeze dry. Add the gelatine once the liquid is boiling. Completely dissolve the gelatine then pass through a fine sieve into a clean bowl and cool over ice, stirring regularly.

While the aspic is still warm pour just enough to cover the bottom into each mould. Allow to set firm in the refrigerator then arrange the mint leaves tidily over the set aspic.

Arrange the orange segments in each mould, leaving a small gap around the edge so that the aspic can sink through. Do not pack the orange segments in too tightly. Once the aspic is cold pour it into each mould. Place them all on a tray and set in the refrigerator for 3 hours.

MELON PURÉE: Place the melon and syrup in a food processor and purée until smooth. Pass through a fine sieve into a clean bowl, pushing as much of the pulp through as possible. Cover and store in the refrigerator.

TO SERVE: Unmould the timbales by dipping each briefly in hot water. Invert the mould, put your fingers underneath, and flick your wrist to release the contents. Place on a plate and divide the purée evenly between each serving. Garnish with melon balls and serve with a glass of champagne.

INGREDIENTS — SERVES 6

8–9	medium-sized oranges
250ml (8½ fl oz)	brut champagne or méthode champenoise
150ml (5 fl oz)	orange juice
1¾ tbsp	castor sugar
4	gelatine leaves
18	small mint leaves
	small melon balls to garnish

MELON PURÉE

200g (7 oz)	rock melon
100ml (3½ fl oz)	sugar syrup (see page 134)

CHOCOLATE MOUSSE WITH SPONGE FINGERS AND SCALDED ORANGE SAUCE

Chocolate and orange make a wonderful combination. This dessert effectively uses fresh and caramelised orange with the chocolate mousse. The sponge fingers are prepared separately and placed around the mousse after it has been turned out. We use 150ml (5 fl oz) moulds and often serve the mousse resting on a disc of chocolate sponge.

INGREDIENTS — SERVES 6

300ml (10 fl oz)	milk
100g (3½ oz)	bitter dark chocolate, finely chopped
5	egg yolks
75g (2½ oz)	castor sugar
4½	gelatine leaves
300ml (10 fl oz)	cream
	orange segments to garnish
	mint to garnish

SPONGE FINGERS

4	egg yolks
90g (3 oz)	castor sugar
3	egg whites
4½ tbsp	cornflour
4 tbsp	flour
	icing sugar for dusting

SAUCE

	zest of 1 orange
150g (5½ oz)	castor sugar
300ml (10 fl oz)	orange juice
60ml	grand marnier (optional)
1 tsp	arrowroot

METHOD: Place the milk in a heavy-bottomed pot with the chocolate and bring to the boil, stirring from time to time.

Whisk the egg yolks and sugar together until pale. Pour one-third of the hot chocolate milk into the egg mixture and stir. Add the egg mixture to the remaining milk then place over a low heat and cook to coating consistency, stirring constantly with a wooden spoon. Do not allow the custard to boil. Remove from the heat.

Soak the gelatine leaves in cold water until soft then squeeze dry. Stir the soaked leaves into the custard until completely dissolved. Pour custard through a fine sieve into a clean bowl then place over a larger bowl of ice to cool.

Lightly whip the cream.

Stir the custard regularly until it just begins to thicken then mix in the cream. Pour into six moulds then cover with plastic wrap and place in the refrigerator to set.

SPONGE FINGERS: Place the egg yolks in a round-bottomed bowl with one-third of the sugar and whisk until pale yellow.

In a separate bowl whisk the egg whites to a soft peak then slowly add the remaining sugar, whisking as you go, until the whites are stiff. Sift the cornflour then carefully fold into the egg whites. Very carefully fold the yolks into the whites. Do not over mix.

Sift the flour into the egg mixture and carefully fold in. The mixture must be quite firm.

Line a baking tray with greaseproof paper or a non-stick teflon sheet.

Fit a size 1 plain piping nozzle into a piping bag. Fill the bag with the mixture then pipe 60–70 fingers measuring 5.5cm x 2cm (2″ x ¾″). Each chocolate mousse will need 10 or 11 fingers.

Lightly dust the raw sponge fingers with icing sugar then place in a pre-heated 190°C (375°F) oven and bake for 8–10 minutes.

While still warm remove from the tray and cool completely on a cake rack. Store in an airtight container.

SAUCE: Place the zest in a small pot and just cover in water. Add a teaspoon of the sugar, then place over a medium heat and cook until the zest is tender.

Place the rest of the sugar in a heavy-bottomed pot then caramelise over a steady heat. Cook to a deep amber colour.

Very carefully add the orange juice and grand marnier a little at a time, stirring constantly. Use a long-handled wooden spoon as there will be a violent reaction when the juice hits the hot toffee. Stir the mixture over a low heat until all the toffee is dissolved. Bring to the boil.

Dissolve the arrowroot in a little water then whisk into the sauce. Simmer for 30 seconds. Pass through a fine sieve into a clean bowl. Add the cooked zest then cover and refrigerate.

TO SERVE: Turn the mousses out of the moulds by briefly dipping in hot water, then shaking out onto the serving plates. Place the sponge fingers around each mousse and put the orange segments on top with a sprig of mint.

Divide the sauce evenly between each portion and serve at room temperature.

RHUBARB PARFAIT WITH MERINGUE WAFERS

Rhubarb is technically a vegetable, although we use it as a fruit. It is thought to be a native of China and is the stem of the plant.

The English can take credit for developing the culinary versatility of rhubarb, for it was they who taught the rest of the world how good rhubarb tarts, pies and jams are.

Rhubarb is well suited to parfaits as its sharp but sweet flavour is not lost with chilling or the addition of cream and eggs. Sandwich the parfait between crunchy meringue wafers and you have a dessert for all occasions.

We use the poaching liquid for the sauce, but a syrup accompanies this dessert very well. You will need a 1.4 litre (3 US pint) terrine mould.

INGREDIENTS — SERVES 8-10

400g (14 oz)	fresh rhubarb
900ml (30 fl oz)	water
360g (12½ oz)	castor sugar
	juice of 1 lemon
	juice of 1 orange
5	egg yolks
300ml (10 fl oz)	cream
2	egg whites
	stewed rhubarb to garnish

MERINGUE

2	large egg whites
50g (1½ oz)	castor sugar
50g (1½ oz)	icing sugar

METHOD: Wash the rhubarb and cut into 2.5cm (1″) lengths. Place in a medium-sized non-reactive pot with the water, 250g (9 oz) of the sugar and the juices. Place over a medium heat and cook until soft.

Remove the rhubarb from the cooking liquid and drain well. Reserve the liquid. Place the rhubarb in a food processor and purée until smooth. Transfer to a clean bowl and chill.

Whisk the egg yolks and the rest of the sugar to ribbon stage, in a large bowl over a bain-marie. Allow to cool, whisking from time to time.

Whip the cream until the whisk leaves tracks.

Whisk the egg whites to a soft peak.

Mix the cold rhubarb purée into the egg yolks and sugar, then mix in the lightly whipped cream. Finally, carefully fold in the beaten egg white. Pour into a terrine mould and freeze.

Reduce the poaching liquid over a steady heat to a syrup. Use this for the sauce.

MERINGUE: In a very clean and dry bowl whisk the egg whites to a soft peak. Gradually whisk in the castor sugar. Once all the sugar is in continue to whisk for 5 minutes. The whites will become firm. Now fold in the sifted icing sugar, a little at a time. Do not over mix.

Line a baking tray witha a non-stick teflon sheet or greaseproof paper. Spread the meringue over the tray, approximately 6mm (¼″) thick, covering an area approximately 30cm (12″) by 26cm (10½″). It doesn't have to be perfect.

Place in a preheated 100°C (210°F) oven and bake until crisp and dry. Keep a very close eye on the meringue as it can colour quickly. This process should take approximately 1½–1¾ hours, but domestic ovens can be inaccurate at lower temperatures. If the meringue is colouring too quickly, cook with the oven door open. Once cooked, cool on a cake rack.

TO SERVE: Take a serrated knife and, using a sawing motion, cut the meringue into 12 even pieces measuring 6.5cm x 8cm (2½″ x 3¼″). Place one on each chilled plate.

Dip the terrine in hot water for the count of 10 then ease the parfait out onto a cutting surface. Slice into even portions then place a slice onto each wafer. Top with the second wafer then garnish with a little stewed rhubarb. Dribble some rhubarb syrup around the plate and serve immediately.

Accompany with rhubarb purée served separately in a sauce boat.

GRAND MARNIER CHARLOTTE WITH MANDARIN

Charlottes are prepared using swiss roll or sponge fingers on the outside and a liqueur cream or bavarois filling.

The filling may be flavoured with one of any number of liqueurs, fruits or flavourings, and may be prepared as one large cake using a basin or special charlotte mould, or as individual portions in 150ml (5 fl oz) dariole moulds.

The small swiss rolls should be prepared in advance then frozen. This enables you to cut the roll more thinly and tidily. The sponge recipe given will provide enough swiss roll for nine charlottes.

INGREDIENTS — SERVES 6

SPONGE

plain sponge
mixture
(see page 136)
strawberry jam for
spreading

LIQUEUR CREAM

250ml (8½ fl oz)	milk
60g (2 oz)	castor sugar
3½	egg yolks
150ml (5 fl oz)	grand marnier
3½	gelatine leaves
250ml (8½ fl oz)	cream

CRÈME ANGLAISE

crème anglaise
(see page 98)

GARNISH

4-5 mandarins

SPONGE: Prepare the sponge mixture according to the instructions on page 136.

Line a baking tray with geaseproof paper then spread the mixture onto the tray. It should measure 40cm x 60cm (16″ x 9½″) and be approximately 4mm (¹/₆″) deep.

Bake in a preheated 180°C (350°F) oven, with the fan on, for 18-20 minutes. Meanwhile, pass the jam through a fine sieve. Thin with a little water if it is not of spreading consistency.

Cut the sponge, with the paper, into three even-sized pieces, cutting across the width of the tray. Place each strip on a damp teatowel, paper side up. Peel off the greaseproof paper then very thinly spread each piece with jam. Do not spread on too much jam or the sponge will be difficult to handle.

Turn the sponge so it is in front of you lengthways then tightly roll it towards you from the top. Repeat with the other two pieces.

Place the swiss rolls in the freezer overnight.

Next day, cut the frozen swiss rolls into slices approximately 4mm (¹/₆″) thick. Line the inside of each mould with slices of swiss roll. Pack them tightly. Trim off any sponge that is above the rim of each mould.

LIQUEUR CREAM: Bring the milk to the boil. Whisk the castor sugar, egg yolks and grand marnier together until pale. Soak the gelatine leaves in cold water until soft then squeeze dry.

Pour the hot milk onto the eggs and sugar and thoroughly mix together. Return to a clean pot, place over a gentle heat and cook to coating consistency, stirring constantly.

Remove from the heat, add the soaked gelatine leaves and mix until they are completely dissolved. Pass the mixture through a fine sieve into a clean bowl then place over ice to cool. Stir regularly.

Lightly whip the cream. When the custard begins to thicken, mix in the cream.

Evenly divide the filling between each lined mould. Place in the refrigerator to set for 1½-2 hours.

CRÈME ANGLAISE: Prepare the crème anglaise according to the instructions on page 98.

TO SERVE: Once the charlottes are set, briefly dip the moulds in hot water then shake the charlottes out. Place in the centre of each serving plate then divide the crème anglaise evenly between each serving. Arrange six mandarin segments on each dish and serve at just below room temperature.

BLUEBERRY TARTE WITH SABRA SYRUP

Blueberries originally grew wild as shrubs that thrived in acidic soils, but they grow well in New Zealand and are used in ice cream, preserves, jams and pies.

This tarte is prepared using fresh blueberries baked in a sweet custard with a golden pâte sablée crust. The syrup is prepared using sabra, a Jaffa orange flavoured liqueur from Israel. You will need a 23cm (9") flan ring. If possible bake the dessert on a rigid baking tray, as a flexible tray may crack the pastry case.

INGREDIENTS — SERVES 6

350g	(12½ oz)	pâte sablée
		(see page 137)
8		eggs
		juice of 1 lemon
175g	(6 oz)	castor sugar
200ml	(7 fl oz)	cream
300g	(10½ oz)	fresh blueberries

SYRUP

150g	(5½ oz)	sugar
175ml	(6 fl oz)	orange juice
100ml	(3½ fl oz)	sabra
1 tsp		arrowroot
		zest of 1 orange
1 tsp		sugar

METHOD: Lightly flour a flat surface and roll out the pâte sablée to a thickness of approximately 4mm (⅛"). Lightly butter a 23cm (9") flan ring and place it on a buttered baking tray.

Carefully line the ring with the pastry. You will have to work quite quickly as the pastry becomes very soft at room temperature. As a general rule, roll it out while it is still quite firm. Patch any holes and cracks in the pastry case, then allow it to firm up in the refrigerator.

Once it is firm, line the pastry case with a circle of greaseproof paper and bake blind by filling with beans or rice. Bake in a preheated 175°C (350°F) oven until the pastry begins to brown around the top rim. Allow it to cool just a little, then remove the paper and beans or rice. Cool the pastry case out of the refrigerator.

Beat just one of the eggs and brush the inside of the pastry case with it. Return the case to the oven for 2–3 minutes to allow the egg wash to set firmly. Repeat this process, then allow the pastry case to cool.

Break the rest of the eggs into a large bowl. Add the lemon juice and sugar, and whisk lightly until well mixed. Add the cream and mix in. Pass the mixture through a fine sieve into a clean bowl to remove any egg shell.

Place the blueberries in the pastry case. Check there are no cracks in the pastry, then fill it with the custard. Bake very slowly in a preheated 100°C (210°F) oven for 1 hour until the egg mixture is set. Remove the tarte from the oven and allow to cool completely at room temperature. Leave the flan ring on and do not cover as this would trap steam and moisten the tart.

SYRUP: Place the sugar in a heavy-bottomed pot and carefully caramelise it to a golden amber colour. Stir from time to time so that it caramelises evenly.

Add the orange juice carefully as the sugar will react violently to the liquid. Cook over a gentle heat until all the toffee has dissolved.

Add the sabra. Bring to the boil then dilute the arrowroot with a little water and whisk it into the syrup. Continue to simmer for 30 seconds. Remove from the heat.

Place the zest in a small pot and just cover with water. Add the teaspoon of sugar and cook the zest until it is tender.

Pass the syrup through a fine sieve into a clean bowl. Add the zest, then cool.

TO SERVE: Dust the tarte with icing sugar, then slice it into six portions. An electric knife is handy for this. Place a slice on a flat plate and spoon on a little syrup and serve.

CALVADOS CREAMS
WITH CARAMELISED APPLE AND SYRUP

This is a classic Huka Lodge dish that uses the ingredient that has made Normandy famous, calvados. The apple spirit is combined with other ingredients such as cream and apples, resulting in a wonderful dessert.

The apples need to be a fresh crisp variety such as Granny Smith or Cox.
The apple used in France for such a dessert is one called Starking or Starking Delicious.

INGREDIENTS — SERVES 6

CREAMS

250ml	(8½ fl oz)	milk
4		egg yolks
60g	(2 oz)	castor sugar
60ml	(2 fl oz)	calvados
3–4		gelatine leaves
150ml	(5 fl oz)	cream

APPLE

3		apples, peeled, cut in half and seeds removed
		clarified butter to sauté
100g	(3½ oz)	castor sugar

SYRUP

100ml	(3½ fl oz)	clear apple concentrate
100ml	(3½ fl oz)	water
100g	(3½ oz)	castor sugar
1 tsp		arrowroot, mixed with a little apple juice

GARNISH

100g	(3½ oz)	melted chocolate for piping
		mint to garnish

CREAMS: Place the milk in a heavy-bottomed pot and bring to the boil. Whisk the egg yolks, sugar and calvados to ribbon stage, when the whisk leaves tracks in the mixture. Pour on a third of the boiling milk and mix. Pour the egg mixture back into the remaining hot milk. Lower the heat and, stirring constantly, cook the custard until it coats the back of a wooden spoon. Remove from the heat.

Soften the gelatine leaves in cold water, squeeze dry then add to the custard. Stir until completely dissolved. Pass through a fine sieve into a clean stainless-steel bowl.

Whip the cream lightly.

Place the custard over a larger bowl of ice and stir until the custard reaches the thickness of unbeaten egg white. Mix in the whipped cream. Pour into a dish or into six to eight 50ml (1¾ fl oz) moulds. Place in the refrigerator and allow to set for at least 2 hours before serving.

APPLE: Cut each apple half into three. Melt a knob of clarified butter in a large sauté pan and toss the apple wedges in it until they just begin to brown. Add the sugar and continue to toss until the sugar begins to caramelise. Toss until they are quite dark. Place on a baking tray with sides, and put aside.

SYRUP: Mix the apple concentrate and water together.

Put the sugar in a heavy-bottomed pot, place over a steady heat and caramelise to a toffee colour. Take off the heat and very carefully add the apple juice. Mix together over a medium heat until the toffee is well mixed in. Thicken with the arrowroot then pass through a fine sieve into a clean bowl. Cover and allow to grow completely cold.

TO SERVE: To create the piped apple, cut an apple-shaped stencil from cardboard. Fit a small piping bag with a fine nozzle and fill with melted chocolate. Hold the stencil steady on the plate with one hand, and pipe around the edge. Pipe on the stem freehand. Keep in a cool place, but not in the refrigerator.

Place the sautéed apples in a warm oven. Briefly dip the cream moulds in warm water then shake them out and position to top left of the prepared plates. Carefully spoon a little of the cold syrup into the apple shape and spread it evenly. Take the warm apple out of the oven and place three wedges on the right hand bottom side of the cream. Garnish the apple with fresh mint and serve.

HAZELNUT GÂTEAU FILLED WITH FRANGELICO LIQUEUR CREAM

This gâteau dates back only a few years to a cooking competition in Rotorua. As on that day, a successful result is always achieved when we serve hazelnut gâteau at Huka Lodge.

The gâteau may be iced with a simple icing sugar/coffee mix, or chocolate, or just dusted with icing sugar.

You will need a 24cm (9½") spring-form cake tin.

INGREDIENTS — MAKES 1

	plain sponge mixture (see page 136)
220g (8 oz)	shelled hazelnuts, ground and toasted
	a little frangelico mixed with sugar syrup (see page 134) to moisten
	whipped cream

LIQUEUR CREAM

5	gelatine leaves
300ml (10 fl oz)	milk
5	egg yolks
75g (2½ oz)	castor sugar
75ml (2½ fl oz)	frangelico
300ml (10 fl oz)	cream

PRALINE

250g (9 oz)	sliced almonds, lightly browned
300g (10½ oz)	castor sugar

METHOD: Make the plain sponge according to the instructions on page 136, but very carefully fold in the ground hazelnuts after the flour and cornflour.

LIQUEUR CREAM: Soak the gelatine leaves in water then squeeze dry.

Bring the milk to the boil. Whisk the egg yolk, sugar and frangelico together to the ribbon stage. Remove the milk from the heat then pour onto the eggs, stirring as you go. Return to a gentle heat, stirring constantly until the mixture coats the back of the wooden spoon. Do not boil.

Remove the custard from the heat then add the soaked gelatine leaves. Stir until completely dissolved, then pass custard through a fine sieve into a clean bowl. Place over ice and chill, stirring regularly.

Lightly whip the cream then mix into the cooled custard.

PRALINE: Roughly chop the lightly browned almonds.

Place the sugar in a pot and melt over a medium-high heat until a pale brown caramel is reached. Stir in the almonds.

Remove praline from heat and pour onto a lightly greased baking tray, spreading or rolling it out until it is approximately 1cm (½") thick. Allow to cool and harden.

Once cold, crush the praline to a fine powder using a meat hammer or rolling pin; cover with a clean cloth to prevent it from going everywhere during crushing.

A food processor will very effectively grind the broken up praline.

SETTING UP: Once the sponge has completely cooled, slice into three layers. Lightly brush the top side of the bottom and middle layers with the liqueur cream. The cream must be a thick pouring consistency. If it is too thin it will leak out, but if it is too thick it won't pour evenly. It may be remelted carefully over a pot of warm water if necessary. Place the bottom slice back in the cake tin. Make sure it is a tight fit. Pour in half the frangelico liqueur cream and spread evenly.

Carefully place the middle layer of sponge in the tin then pour in the remaining liqueur cream, to the top of the cake tin. Put the last layer of sponge on top, cover with plastic wrap, and refrigerate for 2 hours.

Once set remove the cake from the spring-form cake tin, leaving the base under the cake for easier handling. A warm cloth wrapped around the tin may help.

Spread any liqueur cream that has oozed out over the side of the cake and add any leftover, then, using your hand, press the ground praline on the side, so a good coating is achieved. Leave some praline for the garnish. Any leftover liqueur cream may be used up here. Ice or dust the top of the cake as desired.

TO SERVE: Cut into even wedges with a sharp knife or electric knife and serve with freshly whipped cream sprinkled with praline.

HAZELNUT SAXONY PUDDING WITH WARM CHOCOLATE SAUCE

Although this pudding is credited to the English, it has been adopted by both the French and the Germans, resulting in several variations. This is our favourite version and we often serve it with fresh blackberries when in season.

The dessert can be made in eight 100ml (3½ fl oz) moulds or in a loaf tin. It can also be eaten cold, although it will be heavier in the stomach. The recipe may safely be halved.

INGREDIENTS — SERVES 8

100g	(3½ oz)	hazelnuts
100g	(3½ oz)	unsalted butter
100g	(3½ oz)	flour
250ml	(8½ fl oz)	milk
1		vanilla pod
10		egg whites
6		egg yolks
100g	(3½ oz)	castor sugar
		blackberries to
		garnish

CHOCOLATE SAUCE

200g	(7 oz)	dark chocolate
250ml	(8½ fl oz)	cream

METHOD: Roast the hazelnuts then grind quite finely in a blender.

Heat the butter in a medium-sized saucepan. Add the flour and make a roux. Cook over a gentle heat for 6–8 minutes. Do not brown. In another pot bring the milk to the boil with the vanilla pod. Remove the vanilla and beat the milk into the roux a little at a time. Cook over a slow heat until it comes back to the boil, stirring constantly.

Pour the mixture into a clean bowl and allow to cool a little. Beat in 2 egg whites, then mix in the yolks one at a time. Make sure the mixture is smooth before adding the next yolk.

In a clean bowl whip the remaining 8 egg whites to a fluffy snow, slowly adding the sugar as you go. Using a balloon whisk, mix one-third of the snow into the yolk mixture then carefully fold in the remaining snow with a wooden spoon. Finally, very carefully fold in the ground hazelnuts.

Brush all the moulds well with melted butter then dust with castor sugar. Divide the mixture between the moulds, to three-quarters full. Place in a bain-marie and cook in a preheated 180°C (350°F) oven for 25–30 minutes, with the fan on.

CHOCOLATE SAUCE: While the puddings are cooking, finely chop the chocolate then melt in a stainless-steel bowl over a pot of simmering water.

Heat the cream to just below boiling point then quickly mix into the chocolate. Remove from the heat but leave over the pot of hot water.

TO SERVE: Remove the puddings from the oven and allow to stand for 15–20 seconds. Carefully remove from the moulds with the aid of a thin sharp knife.

Place in the middle of a luncheon plate or rimmed soup bowl. Pour the warm chocolate sauce around and garnish with fresh blackberries. Serve immediately.

STUFFED APPLES WITH SABLÉ
AND CRÈME ANGLAISE

In this dish we generally use Royal Gala, Granny Smith or Golden Delicious apples, as they keep their shape when cooked. There is no need to peel the apples — the skin helps hold things together, and once the apples are cooked the skin is easy to remove should you not wish to eat it.

METHOD: Prepare the pâte sablée according to the instructions on page 137. Roll out to 3mm (¹/₈″) thick on a flat floured surface. Using a 7cm (2¾″) plain cutter, cut out 12 biscuits. Place on a baking tray and bake in a preheated 200°C (400°F) oven for 5-6 minutes.

Cool on a cake rack and store in an airtight container.

Prepare the crème anglaise according to the instructions on page 98. Cover and refrigerate until required.

Place six of the apples the right way up then cut one-third off the top. If necessary cut a little apple from the base to make it sit flat. Using a melon baller, remove the seeds, making a cavity large enough to hold the filling. Do not go right through the apple.

Place the apples in a buttered roasting tin, cavity side up. Sprinkle with 2½ tbsp of the castor sugar. Pour approximately 150ml (5 fl oz) of water in the tray, then place in a preheated 200°C (400°F) oven for 10 minutes.

While the apples are cooking, peel, core and grate the rest of the apples. Combine the grated apple, remaining sugar, zest, cream, egg yolks, salt and cinnamon in a bowl.

After removing the apples from the oven, pour out any juice then fill each apple with stuffing. Pile the filling up as high as possible then evenly sprinkle with brown sugar. Dot with butter then return to the 200°C (400°F) oven and bake for 20-25 minutes, until brown.

TO SERVE: The apples may be eaten warm or cold. Place one sablé biscuit on each flat plate and lightly dust with icing sugar, then place the apple on top. Divide the sauce evenly around the apple. Dust the remaining sablé with cinnamon then arrange against the apple and serve.

INGREDIENTS — SERVES 6

	pâte sablée (see page 137)
	crème anglaise (see page 98)
8-9	medium-sized apples
100g (3½ oz)	castor sugar
	zest of 2 small lemons, finely chopped
60ml (2 fl oz)	cream
3	egg yolks
	pinch of salt
½ tsp	ground cinnamon
	brown sugar for sprinkling
30g (1 oz)	unsalted butter
	icing sugar for dusting
	cinnamon for dusting

CHOCOLATE TRUFFLE TARTE

The beauty of this dessert is that it will last several days if kept well covered in the refrigerator.

It is important to use good quality chocolate as this is the main ingredient. We use Belgian chocolate which is available from good kitchen shops and delicatessens.

In this recipe the chocolate truffle tarte is served with orange crème anglaise, but it may also be served with a red berry coulis. For the sponge base you will need a 25cm (10″) flan ring or spring-form cake tin. This recipe will serve 12-14 people, but it may safely be halved.

INGREDIENTS — SERVES 12-14

SPONGE

200g	(7 oz)	castor sugar
8		eggs
100g	(3½ oz)	cocoa
100g	(3½ oz)	flour
		nip of rum
100ml	(3½ fl oz)	sugar syrup
		(see page 134)

CHOCOLATE TRUFFLE

450g	(1 lb)	dark chocolate
650ml	(22 fl oz)	cream

CRÈME ANGLAISE

10		egg yolks
200g	(7 oz)	castor sugar
60ml	(2 fl oz)	orange juice
900ml	(30 fl oz)	milk
½		vanilla pod

GARNISH

4-5	oranges

SPONGE: Whisk the sugar and eggs together until they are pale in colour and start to form a peak when the whisk is lifted.

Sieve the cocoa and the flour together then carefully fold into the sugar and egg mixture.

Brush a 25cm (10″) cake tin or flan ring with soft butter then dust with flour. Shake off excess flour. Carefully and evenly pour the sponge mixture into the tin. Place in a preheated 190 °C (375 °F) oven for 5 minutes then turn the oven down to 160 °C (310 °F) and cook for another 10–15 minutes. While the sponge is still warm remove it from the tin and place it on a cake rack to completely cool.

Place the cooled sponge on a flat surface then, using a long bread knife, slice the sponge in half, cutting across the sponge. You will need a slice approximately 1.5cm (¾″) thick.

Clean the flan ring or cake tin and place it on a baking tray. Place half of the sponge in the bottom of the tin, with the freshly cut side up. The remaining half of the sponge can be frozen to use later for the same dessert. Mix the rum and sugar syrup together, then evenly moisten the top of the sponge.

Put aside until required.

CHOCOLATE TRUFFLE: Finely chop the chocolate and place it in a large bowl over a pot of simmering water. Completely melt the chocolate, stirring it from time to time and making sure it does not get too hot. Remove the pot, with the bowl of melted chocolate still attached, from the heat.

Very lightly whisk the cream so it only slightly thickens then mix it into the warm chocolate, stirring quickly as you go. Continue to mix until the cream is evenly incorporated.

While the chocolate truffle is still warm pour it onto the sponge base in the tin. Spread the chocolate evenly then lightly tap the tin twice to settle the mixture.

Place in the refrigerator for a minimum of 4 hours before serving.

CRÈME ANGLAISE: Place the egg yolks in a large bowl with the sugar and orange juice. Whisk them together until the whisk leaves definite tracks in the mixture.

Place the milk and vanilla pod in a heavy-bottomed pot over a medium heat then bring it to just on boiling point. Remove the vanilla pod. Pour the hot milk onto the egg mixture, stirring with a wooden spoon as you pour.

Pour the custard back into a clean pot then place it over a low heat, stirring constantly with a wooden spoon, until the custard will coat the back of the spoon. Pass the crème anglaise through a fine sieve into a clean stainless-steel bowl and cool, stirring every so often.

If you think the crème anglaise is too hot and may overcook, place the bowl straight into a larger bowl of ice. It may pay to have a bowl of ice on standby.

TO SERVE: Wrap a hot teatowel around the cake tin or flan ring until it loosens from the chocolate truffle tarte, then remove the tin. Cut the truffle tarte into wedges and place each one on a cold place. Spoon a puddle of cold crème anglaise next to the wedge. Garnish each wedge with three orange segments and serve.

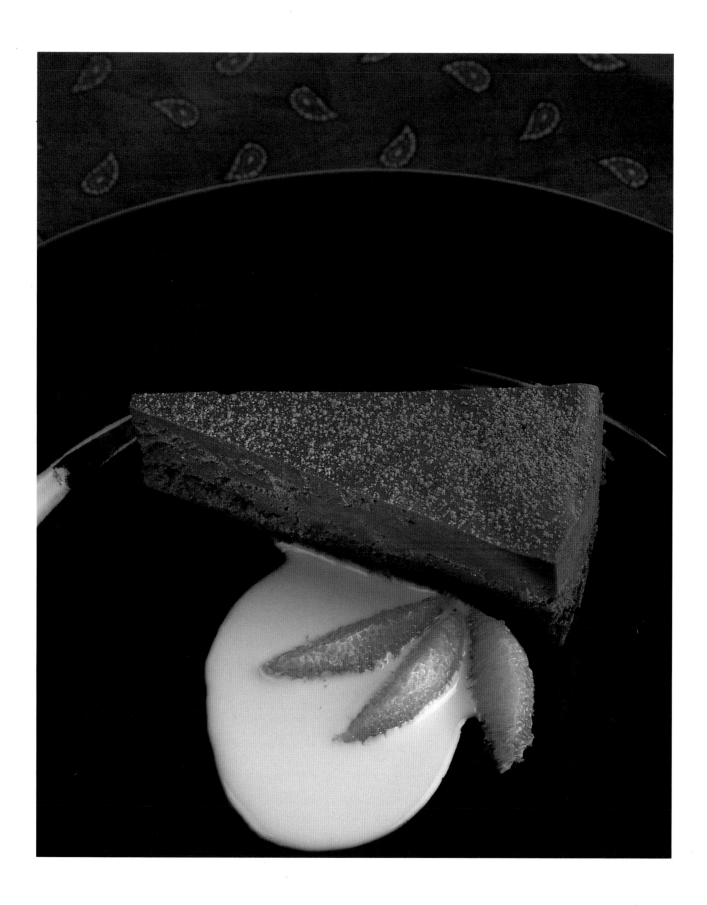

LEMON SOUFFLÉ WITH LEMON BUTTER SAUCE

Prepared since the turn of the century, the soufflé continues to delight diners around the world. Is it because they are aware of the split-second timing required in presenting a successful soufflé, or is it the near weightlessness in the mouth, or is it just taste?

It may be a little tense waiting for the soufflé to rise evenly and the tendency to deflate rapidly certainly does not help, but there is a great feeling of achievement long after a successful soufflé has disappeared into the dining room.

INGREDIENTS — SERVES 6-7

375ml	(12½ fl oz)	milk
80g	(3 oz)	castor sugar
4½		egg yolks
55g	(2 oz)	flour
		icing sugar for dusting
210ml	(7 fl oz)	lemon juice
		zest of 4 lemons, finely chopped

LEMON BUTTER SAUCE

90ml	(3 fl oz)	lemon juice
90ml	(3 fl oz)	cream
50g	(1½ oz)	castor sugar
150g	(5½ oz)	unsalted butter

SNOW

9	egg whites
1 tbsp	castor sugar

METHOD: Brush six 150ml (5 fl oz) ramekins liberally with soft butter, making sure the entire inside surface is coated. Dust with castor sugar, coating evenly. Lightly tap out any excess sugar and keep in a cool place until required.

Place the milk in a pot with 2 tbsp of the sugar then bring to the boil.

Beat egg yolks with the rest of the sugar in a large bowl until pale. Sift in flour and beat together.

Pour the hot milk into the egg mixture a little at a time, stirring constantly. Transfer to a clean pot and bring back to the boil over a gentle heat, stirring with a wooden spoon. Simmer for 1½ minutes, continuing to beat.

Place this soufflé mixture in a large stainless steel bowl and allow to cool to lukewarm.

Put the lemon juice in a non-reactive pot and reduce to 80ml (2½ fl oz). Add the chopped zest just before the juice has reduced to the required amount. Beat the lemon mixture into the lukewarm soufflé mixture. Cover the bowl to prevent a skin forming then cool to room temperature.

LEMON BUTTER SAUCE: Mix the lemon juice with the cream then, over a gentle heat, reduce by two-thirds. Mix in the sugar, stirring until it has dissolved.

Over a very gentle heat slowly whisk in the butter a little at a time. Pour into a sauce boat, cover and keep lukewarm.

SNOW: Beat the egg whites in an electric mixer until fluffy then add the sugar in batches. Beat to a soft peak.

TO COOK AND SERVE: When you are ready to bake the soufflé, mix a quarter of the snow into the soufflé mixture to lighten it up and make it more receptive to the rest of the snow. Carefully fold in the remaining snow with a large spoon, being careful not to over mix. The air in the snow must not be lost.

Evenly fill the prepared ramekins right to the top. Smooth the top with a palette knife or spatula. Clean the rims and sides of the ramekins.

Place the soufflés on a baking tray, making sure they are well spaced. Cook in a preheated 180°C (350°F) oven for 15-17 minutes, with the fan on.

While the soufflés are cooking make sure all the serving plates and accompaniments are organised. If possible have someone to help you.

Once cooked, remove the soufflés from the oven. Dust with icing sugar, place on the serving plates and serve absolutely immediately.

Have the tepid butter sauce on the table waiting. Each diner can cut a hole in the top of their soufflé and pour some in.

WARM SUMMER BERRIES GRATINATED WITH CARAMEL SABAYON, SERVED WITH RUM AND RAISIN ICE CREAM AND ORANGE TUILES

This dish is very simple to prepare and delicious to eat. The combination of berries is entirely up to you, although the following combination gives the best result.

The berries taste better after a minimum of 24 hours in the marinade, so you will need to prepare them the day before they are required. They will last up to three days and taste better as each day goes by. This is a warm dish, not a hot one.

INGREDIENTS — SERVES 6

720g	(1¼ lb)	mixed berries (strawberries, blueberries, raspberries, blackberries)
100ml	(3½ fl oz)	sugar syrup (see page 134)
2 tbsp		dark rum

TUILES

60g	(2 oz)	unsalted butter
2		egg whites
110g	(3¾ oz)	castor sugar
		pinch salt
60g	(2 oz)	flour
1½ tbsp		very finely chopped orange zest

CARAMEL SABAYON

150g	(5½ oz)	castor sugar
150ml	(5 fl oz)	cream
4		egg yolks
		splash of sugar syrup

RUM AND RAISIN ICE CREAM

6		egg yolks
250g	(9 oz)	castor sugar
500ml	(17 fl oz)	milk
½		vanilla pod
600ml	(20 fl oz)	cream
150g		raisins, soaked and chopped
175ml	(6 fl oz)	dark rum
		mint to garnish

METHOD: Hull and quarter the strawberries, and carefully wash the remaining berries and pat dry.

Purée 60g (2 oz) of the blackberries and 60g (2 oz) of the raspberries then place in a large bowl. Mix in the sugar syrup then the rum. Add the prepared berries to the marinade and carefully mix in. Cover and place in the refrigerator for 24 hours.

TUILES: Place all the ingredients except the orange zest in a bowl or food processor and mix until very smooth. Then add the zest.

Liberally brush a baking tray with butter then dust with flour. Tap off excess flour. Cook the tuiles in batches of four to six. Mark out 10 cm (4") circles then thinly spread the batter to the marked size. Cook in a preheated 190°C (375°F) oven for 3–5 minutes, until dark brown round the edges and golden in the centre.

Remove from the oven and, while still hot, use a flexible palette knife to remove the tuiles from the tray. Wrap them around a rolling pin and allow to cool completely. When cool, carefully remove the tuiles and store in an airtight container.

CARAMEL SABAYON: Place sugar in a heavy-bottomed pot and caramelise to rich and quite dark caramel. Remove from the heat. Heat the cream to just below boiling point then carefully add the caramel mixture and combine. Stir until all the caramel is dissolved. Cover and put aside, but do not refrigerate.

Put the yolks in a basin and add a splash of sugar syrup. Cover and put aside.

RUM AND RAISIN ICE CREAM: Beat egg yolks and sugar together.

Bring milk to the boil with the vanilla pod. Remove the vanilla pod, pour the hot milk into the egg yolks and mix together. Return to a moderate heat and cook to a coating consistency, stirring constantly. Pass through a fine sieve into a cold bowl.

Lightly whip the cream and add to the custard. Allow to cool completely. Add soaked and chopped raisins and the rum.

Freeze using an ice cream machine, in batches if necessary.

TO SERVE: Evenly divide the marinated berries between six ovenproof ramekins or small bowls, being sure to serve with a little of the marinade.

Whisk the sabayon over a bain-marie to ribbon stage, when the whisk leaves tracks. Pour in the caramel, whisking as you go. Be careful not to over beat. You may need to thin the caramel with a little hot water.

Spoon plenty of sabayon over each bowl of berries then place under a hot grill and brown. Watch carefully as the sabayon will burn very quickly. Put the bowls on a baking tray and place in a warm oven to lightly heat through.

Serve immediately with rum and raisin ice cream and orange tuiles.

BLACK BUN WITH GINGER SAUCE

The name of this dish is quite misleading, as this is in fact a traditional rich Scottish fruit cake, normally served at Hogmanay.

It should be prepared several weeks before it is required, so that the flavours can mature.

If kept airtight in a cool, dark place this cake will keep for up to a year. Owing to the long cooking and maturing time, we generally only prepare this cake for Christmas and New Year, serving it with a creamy ginger crème anglaise in a separate sauce boat. The sauce may be served either cold or warm. You will need a 20-23cm (8-9") square tin.

INGREDIENTS — MAKES 1

CASING DOUGH

225g	(8 oz)	flour
100g	(3½ oz)	unsalted butter
½ tsp	(2-3½ fl oz)	water
		beaten egg for egg wash

CAKE

900g	(2 lb)	raisins
1.4kg	(3 lb)	currants
225g	(8 oz)	chopped, blanched almonds
160g	(5½ oz)	flour
225g	(8 oz)	castor sugar
2 tsp		allspice
1 tsp		ground ginger
1 tsp		ground cinnamon
4		black peppercorns, finely crushed
1 tsp		cream of tartar
1 tsp		baking powder
1 tbsp		brandy
100ml	(3½ fl oz)	milk

GINGER SAUCE

50g	(1½ oz)	fresh ginger
100g	(3½ oz)	castor sugar
6		egg yolks
450ml	(15 fl oz)	milk

CASING DOUGH: Combine the flour and baking powder in a large bowl. Cut up the butter then rub into the flour. Mix to a stiff paste with the water.

Turn out onto a floured surface and roll into a smooth ball. Do not over work or the dough will become tough and hard to roll out. Square off the ball. Reserve approximately 150g (5½ oz) of the dough for the lid, then roll out the remainder into a thin sheet.

Brush the tin with butter and dust with flour. Shake off the excess flour then line the tin with the dough. Make sure the dough comes to the top of the tin and overlaps a little to make attaching the lid easier.

CAKE: Mix together all the ingredients except the milk.

Add the milk a little at a time until the mixture is just moist. Place the filling in the lined tin.

Roll out the dough for the lid. Moisten the edges of the lid and tin lining with egg wash then put the lid on top. Press together as well as possible. Prick all over with a fork then, using a skewer, make four holes right down to the bottom of the cake

Bake in a preheated 100°C (210°F) oven for 2½-3 hours. If the cake colours too much cover with aluminium foil.

Allow to cool completely in the tin before turning out. Store in an airtight container.

GINGER SAUCE: Peel the ginger then cut into fine julienne strips. Place in a small pot and just cover with water. Add a teaspoon of the sugar then cook over a gentle heat until just tender. Strain off the water.

Whisk the egg yolks and the rest of the sugar together until pale yellow.

Bring the milk to the boil then add to the eggs and sugar, stirring as you pour. Pour the custard back into the pot then continue to cook over a gentle heat, stirring constantly until the sauce coats the back of the wooden spoon. Do not boil.

Pass through a fine sieve into a clean bowl. Add the ginger and allow to cool, stirring from time to time. Cover and place in the refrigerator.

TO SERVE: Cut into pieces as required. Serve dusted with icing sugar and the sauce on the side.

GRAPE LIQUEUR FLAN WITH SAUTERNES GLAZE

The grape is one of the oldest cultivated plants. The original vines grew up the trunks of trees on the southern shores of the Caspian Sea. From there, it was into southwestern Asia and on to Greece. However, it was the Romans who spread the vine through Europe.

In this recipe we use a 26cm (10½") flan ring which is 4.5cm (1¾") deep. This yields 10-12 portions. This recipe may safely be halved. The flan will keep for a couple of days if well covered and refrigerated.

INGREDIENTS — SERVES 10-12

SPONGE

	plain sponge mixture (see page 136)

LIQUEUR CREAM

5	gelatine leaves
300ml (10 fl oz)	milk
5	egg yolks
75g (2½ oz)	castor sugar
75ml (2½ fl oz)	fruity dessert wine
300ml (10 fl oz)	cream
60-70	red and green grapes, halved and seeded

GLAZE

150g (5½ oz)	castor sugar
400ml (13½ fl oz)	sauternes
	juice of 3 lemons
1 tsp	arrowroot

GARNISH

80-100	grapes, halved and seeded

SPONGE: Prepare the sponge mixture according to the instructions on page 136.

Line a flat baking tray with greaseproof paper then spread the sponge mixture over an area of approximately 40cm x 50cm (16" x 20"). The mixture should be approximately 4mm (¹/₆") deep.

Place in a preheated 180°C (350°C) oven, with the fan on, and bake until the mixture sets, about 20 minutes. Cool a little then remove from the tray and place on a cutting surface.

Peel off the greaseproof paper then cut a 26cm (10½") diameter circle for the base and sufficient 4.5cm (1¾") wide strips for the sides.

Place the flan ring on a flat board then insert the sponge base into the ring. Make sure the base fits tightly. Line the sides of the ring with the strips of sponge, making sure any joins are tightly butted together. Put aside.

LIQUEUR CREAM: Soak the gelatine leaves in water then squeeze dry. Bring the milk to the boil.

Whisk the egg yolk, sugar and dessert wine together to the ribbon stage.

Remove the milk from the heat then pour onto the eggs, stirring as you go. Return to a gentle heat, stirring constantly with a wooden spoon until the mixture coats the back of the spoon. Do not boil.

Remove custard from heat then add the soaked gelatine leaves. Stir until completely dissolved, then pass through a fine sieve into a clean bowl. Place over ice and chill, stirring regularly.

Lightly whip the cream then mix into the cooled custard. Once the liqueur cream begins to thicken, mix in the prepared grapes.

Pour into the lined flan ring. Place in the refrigerator to set for approximately 2 hours.

GLAZE: Place the sugar, sauternes and juice in a pot. Dilute the arrowroot in a little water. Bring the sugary liquid to the boil then whisk in the arrowroot. Simmer for 1 minute. Pass through a fine sieve into a bowl. Cover and refrigerate.

TO SERVE: Using an electric knife, cut the flan into wedges. Wipe the knife blades between each slice.

Carefully lay a wedge on each plate. Arrange the grapes around the wedge then divide the glaze evenly between each portion. Serve just below room temperature.

RUM AND RAISIN CHEESECAKE

Cheesecake has been prepared for centuries. Although they did not invent it, the Romans refined and developed the dish.

Cheesecake was very popular in seventeenth and eighteenth century Great Britain, and it was later introduced to the USA by Russian and Polish immigrants.

Most, if not all, of the early cheesecakes were baked and contained flour, curd and honey. Our recipe is the modern version and does not require cooking. This recipe makes one cheesecake in a 26cm (10½") flan ring or tin, 5cm (2") deep.

Cheesecake will keep well if covered and refrigerated. This recipe may safely be halved. The raisins are soaked in the rum overnight then the rum is strained off and used to melt the gelatine and flavour the cheesecake.

INGREDIENTS — SERVES 12-14

BASE

230g (8 oz)	wholemeal digestive biscuits
1 tsp	cocoa
4 tbsp	golden syrup
60g (2 oz)	unsalted butter

FILLING

450g (1 lb)	cream cheese
150g (5½ oz)	icing sugar
6-7	gelatine leaves
200g (7 oz)	raisins, chopped and soaked overnight in rum
300ml (10 fl oz)	dark rum to soak raisins
750ml (25 fl oz)	cream

GARNISH

	chocolate fans (optional) (see page 131) icing sugar for dusting whipped cream

BASE: Finely crush the biscuits then mix in the cocoa.

Melt the golden syrup and butter together over a gentle heat then combine with the biscuit. Mix together well and allow to firm up, then place a 26cm (10½") flan ring on a baking tray lined with greaseproof paper and press the mixture into the ring to form the base. Compact then allow to set.

FILLING: Beat the cream cheese until soft then sift in the icing sugar, mixing until smooth.

Soak the gelatine leaves until soft then squeeze out any excess water.

Strain the rum from the raisins into a small pot. Add the soaked gelatine leaves then dissolve over a very gentle heat. Remove from heat but keep warm.

Whip the cream until just under ribbon stage.

Mix the raisins into the cheese mix. Pass the gelatine and rum mixture through a fine sieve into the cheese mixture and thoroughly beat together. Fold into the lightly whipped cream, making sure it is well blended.

Pour the mixture into the flan ring over the prepared base. Tap the filling down to ensure there are no air bubbles or caps. Use a rubber spatula to help.

Place in the refrigerator to set for 3-4 hours.

TO SERVE: Cut the cheesecake into wedges. Garnish with chocolate fans (see page 131) then lightly dust with icing sugar. Serve with whipped cream.

Red berry coulis or orange crème anglaise are also good accompaniments to this cheesecake.

SUMMER BERRY FEUILLETÉ WITH SABAYON

Generally this dessert only features on our menu in summer, when the fruit is at its best, its fruity sweetness developed by nature, not hydroponics. The raspberries should be firm and have a slightly matt appearance. The blueberries should also be firm with a bloom similar to that of a grape, and the strawberries must be deep red right through, firm and shiny.

In this dessert we combine crunchy caramelised filo wafers with the berries, then link it all together with a light sabayon.

METHOD: Cut 24 rectangles measuring 7cm x 9cm (2¾″ x 3½″) from a double layer of filo made by brushing one sheet with melted butter and folding over. Carefully lay rectangles on a baking tray lined with a non-stick teflon sheet. Evenly dust with icing sugar, then place under a hot grill. Watch carefully and remove when the sugar has caramelised and the filo is golden all over. Allow to cool.

Purée the 200g (7 oz) strawberries, adding the sugar syrup as you go. Pass through a fine sieve into a clean bowl. Cut the 27 strawberries in half and toss in the coulis.

Place one caramelised filo wafer in the middle of each plate and put nine strawberry halves on the wafer. Put another wafer on top and arrange 12 blueberries on it, then spoon over a little coulis. Repeat with another wafer, 12 raspberries and a little more coulis.

SABAYON: Place all the sabayon ingredients in a round-bottomed bowl then place over a pot of simmering water. Whisk the mixture with a balloon whisk until it is pale yellow and doubled in quantity.

TO SERVE: Evenly spoon the sabayon around each feuilleté, garnish with mint and serve immediately.

INGREDIENTS — SERVES 6

		filo pastry
		icing sugar for dusting
200g	(7 oz)	strawberries for coulis
27		medium-sized strawberries
72		whole blueberries
72		whole raspberries
100ml	(3½ fl oz)	sugar syrup (see page 134)

SABAYON

		mint to garnish
5		egg yolks
75g	(2½ oz)	castor sugar
60ml	(2 fl oz)	cointreau

VANILLA BAVAROIS WITH APPLE PURÉE AND CHOCOLATE GANACHE

This simple yet elegant dessert is one of our favourites. Bavarois (a form of custard), apple and chocolate make a great combination.

We use 100ml (3½ fl oz) moulds to make the presentation more attractive, but the bavarois may be set in any suitable container. The purée, bavarois and garnish may all be prepared in advance.

INGREDIENTS — SERVES 6

BAVAROIS

1	vanilla pod, split
250ml (8½ fl oz)	milk
4	egg yolks
60g (2 oz)	castor sugar
4	gelatine leaves
150ml (5 fl oz)	cream
1	egg white

APPLE PURÉE

5–6	medium-sized stewing apples
2½ tsp	castor sugar
	juice of 1 lemon
	sugar syrup (see page 134)

GANACHE

200g (7 oz)	dark chocolate
100ml (3½ fl oz)	cream

GARNISH

2.5cm (1″)	discs of caramelised apple (optional)
18	small meringues (optional)
	icing sugar for dusting

BAVAROIS: Place the split vanilla pod in the milk and bring to the boil in a heavy-bottomed pot.

Whisk the egg yolks with the sugar until doubled in quantity. Pour one-third of the hot milk onto the egg yolks and mix together with a wooden spoon. Pour the egg mixture back into the remaining milk.

Lower the heat and cook, stirring constantly, until the custard coats the back of a wooden spoon. Remove from the heat. Pass through a sieve into a cold bowl to cool.

Soften the gelatine leaves in cold water and squeeze dry, then add to the custard. Stir until completely dissolved. Pass the custard through a fine sieve into a large, clean stainless-steel bowl.

Lightly whip the cream and beat the egg white to a fluffy snow.

Place the custard over a large bowl of ice and chill. Stir constantly until the custard just begins to thicken. Mix in the cream, then carefully fold in the egg white.

Pour into the moulds or a dish. Refrigerate for 2 hours.

APPLE PURÉE: Peel, core then thinly slice the apples. Place in a non-reactive pot with a little water, the sugar and the juice. Cook over a medium-low heat until soft, stirring regularly.

Cool a little then purée in a food processor or liquidiser. Add sugar syrup a little at a time during this process, until the purée is just pouring consistency, not too thick.

Transfer to a clean bowl, cover with plastic wrap and store in the refrigerator.

GANACHE: Chop the chocolate then melt in a bowl over a pot of simmering water. Bring the cream to the boil then add it to the chocolate. Mix together thoroughly. Remove from the heat and allow to cool at room temperature, stirring regularly, until a smooth piping consistency is reached.

TO SERVE: Release the edges of each bavarois with a knife. Briefly dip each mould into hot water then shake out onto a chilled serving plate.

Spoon the apple purée around, then form three quenelles of ganache and place on each plate.

Garnish with the optional extras as illustrated and serve at room temperature.

CARAMELISED PEAR TARTE

This is a tarte that has proven very popular at Huka Lodge. Preparing it is a long but not difficult process. Winter Cole pears are best, but other varieties will do when these are not available.

You will need to make this tarte in the morning as it is eaten at room temperature and requires several hours to cool properly. Try to avoid putting it in the refrigerator because, as with most egg-based desserts, the flavours are inhibited by over cooling.

Leftover tarte will last for a couple of days if kept well covered in the refrigerator, but the flavour may not be as good. We use a 25cm (10") flan ring but if you do not have one that size this recipe may safely be halved.

INGREDIENTS — SERVES 8-10

500g	(1 lb 2 oz)	pâte sablée (see page 137)
		beaten eggs for brushing
6-7		firm, medium-sized pears
		clarified butter to sauté
150g	(5½ oz)	castor sugar
		icing sugar for dusting

FILLING

10		eggs
		juice of 1 lemon
175g	(6½ oz)	castor sugar
250ml	(8½ fl oz)	cream

CITRUS SYRUP

		zest of 1 lime
		zest of 1 lemon
		zest of ½ orange
50g	(1½ oz)	castor sugar
150ml	(5 fl oz)	orange juice
100ml	(3½ fl oz)	lemon juice
3½ tbsp		lime juice
1 tsp		arrowroot

METHOD: Lightly flour a flat surface and roll out the pâte sablée to approximately 4mm (⅙"). Line the flan ring or case with the pastry. Do not allow it to become too soft or warm or the pastry will become impossible to work with.

Rest the pastry case in the refrigerator for 15 minutes, then line it with a circle of greaseproof paper and fill with beans or rice. Bake blind in a pre-heated 175-180°C (330-350°F) oven for 15-20 minutes.

Remove the greaseproof paper and beans or rice and allow the case to cool slightly.

Thoroughly brush the inside of the pastry case with beaten egg. Return to the oven and cook until the layer of egg sets. Brush again with egg and cook until it sets.

Peel and quarter the pears, keeping them in acidulated water to prevent browning.

Using a large sauté pan over a high heat, melt a little clarified butter. Pat the pears with a paper towel to dry then carefully add half the pears or less, depending on the size of your pan. Toss a couple of times then sprinkle over some of the sugar, leaving enough for the next batch of pears. Continue to toss the pears in sugar until the sugar begins to caramelise and the pears turn a rich brown. Do not overcook the pears, they should be just firm.

Allow to cool on a tray.

FILLING: Combine the eggs, lemon juice, 75g (2½ oz) of the sugar and 50ml (1½ fl oz) of the cream in a large stainless-steel bowl. Mix together well then pass through a fine sieve into a clean bowl.

Caramelise the rest of the sugar until quite dark then remove from the heat and very carefully add the remaining cream a little at a time until well mixed in. Once the caramel has cooled, mix it into the custard.

TO COOK AND SERVE: Fan the caramelised pears around the outside of the flan case then slowly pour in the custard. Cook in a preheated 160°C (310°F) oven for 15-20 minutes, with the fan on. Turn the oven down to 100°C (210°F) and cook for another 1½-1¾ hours, with the fan off, until firm. The custard should be set. Allow to cool at room temperature.

CITRUS SYRUP: Place the zest in a small pot with just enough water to cover and add a pinch of the sugar. Reduce over a steady heat until all the liquid has gone. Allow to cool.

Put the rest of the sugar and the fruit juice in a pot and bring to the boil. Dilute the arrowroot with a little water and whisk into the syrup. Simmer for 3 minutes. Pass through a fine sieve onto the zest and mix together. Place in a clean bowl and allow to cool completely.

Place a wedge of pear tarte in the middle of a flat plate. Dust with icing sugar. Pour a small pool of citrus syrup next to the tarte and serve immediately.

APPLE CRUMBLE WITH BLACKBERRIES AND CREAM

Apple crumble has been around for some time. It has always been one of our favourites so, needless to say, the guests at Huka Lodge now enjoy our version of the not so humble, apple crumble.

In this recipe we use a 26cm (10½") flan ring, which is 5cm (2") deep. The recipe will either double or be halved quite safely. Use apples that do not stew too much once cooked, such as Braeburn.

INGREDIENTS — SERVES 10-12

575g (1¼ lb)	short sweet pastry or pâte sablée (see page 137)
2.2kg (4¾ lb)	apples
	zest of 1½ oranges
	generous pinch of ground cinnamon
3	cloves
	sugar to taste
75g (2½ oz)	unsalted butter
100g (3½ oz)	flour
75g (2½ oz)	brown sugar
1½ tsp	grated or very finely chopped fresh ginger
	fresh blackberries or kerriberries
	whipped cream

METHOD: Roll the pastry out to 4mm (¹⁄₆"). Line the flan ring or oven-proof dish with pastry and rest in the refrigerator for 15 minutes. Line with a circle of greaseproof paper and fill with beans or rice. Bake in a preheated 175-180°C (330-350°F) oven for 15-20 minutes. Discard the paper and beans or rice.

Peel the apples then cut into even wedges, approximately six per apple. Cut out the seeds and place in a large non-reactive pot. Add the zest, cinnamon and cloves then place over a gentle heat. Cover with a lid and cook until the apples are soft. Stir the apples from time to time to prevent colouring. Try not to break the apple up. Add sugar to taste if necessary.

Once cooked drain off the excess liquid and cool the apples. Pack quite firmly into the pastry case.

Rub the butter into the flour to a sandy texture. Mix in the brown sugar and ginger. Evenly spread over the top of the apple.

Place the crumble in a preheated 170°C (325°F) oven, with the fan on, and bake until the crumble is well browned, about 25 minutes. Make sure the pastry doesn't become too dark.

TO SERVE: The crumble may be served warm or cold. Cut into portions with a sharp knife or electric knife and serve with lots of fresh berries and whipped cream.

LECHE FRITA

The Basques, who consider themselves the leaders of Spanish gastronomy, are the creators of this simple dessert. We have merely altered it to suit our taste, by accompanying the 'milk fritters' with cinnamon iced soufflé and a fruit purée such as peach, apricot or red berry.

You will need to make the iced soufflé the day or the morning before.

ICED SOUFFLÉ: Whisk the egg yolks, sugar and cinnamon to the ribbon stage in a large bowl over a bain-marie. Ensure all the sugar dissolves. Allow to cool, whisking regularly.

Whisk the cream until the whisk leaves tracks.

Whisk the egg whites until fluffy.

Fold the cream into the yolk and sugar mixture, ensuring it is evenly mixed in. Carefully fold in the egg whites. Do not over mix or tap the container as that will knock the air out.

Pour into a suitable container and freeze.

FRUIT PURÉE: Blend the fresh fruit in a food processor or liquidiser, adding the sugar syrup as you go. Pass through a fine sieve into a clean bowl. Cover with plastic wrap and place in the refrigerator until required.

FRITA: Mix the cornflour, flour and sugar together then dilute with 125ml (3½ fl oz) of the milk.

Place the rest of the milk, the vanilla, cinnamon and zest in a pot and bring to the boil. Lower the heat then slowly simmer for 2 minutes.

Pass the milk through a fine sieve into a clean pot. Slowly pour the flour, sugar and milk mixture into the hot milk, stirring as you go. Place over a medium heat and stir back to the boil. Allow to simmer for 2 minutes. Pour into a flat tray to approximately 1cm (½″) deep. Allow to cool completely.

Once the mixture is cold and set, cut into 12 even squares. Dip each square in beaten egg then in flour. Shake off the excess flour.

Heat the oil then quickly fry until crisp and golden on both sides. Lightly roll each square in castor sugar and keep warm until required.

TO SERVE: Place a pool of the fruit purée on a cold flat plate then place a ball of the iced soufflé on the purée. Put two of the warm milk fritters next to the soufflé, garnish with a sprig of mint and serve immediately.

INGREDIENTS — SERVES 6

ICED SOUFFLÉ

5		egg yolks
110g	(4 oz)	castor sugar
2 tsp		ground cinnamon
300ml	(10 fl oz)	cream
2		egg whites

FRUIT PURÉE

150g	(5½ oz)	fresh fruit
100ml	(3½ fl oz)	sugar syrup (see page 134)

FRITA

50g	(1½ oz)	cornflour
50g	(1½ oz)	flour
200g	(7 oz)	castor sugar
1 litre	(34 fl oz)	milk
1		vanilla pod, split
1		cinnamon stick
		zest of 1 lemon
2		eggs, beaten
		flour for coating
		vegetable oil for frying
		castor sugar for dusting
		mint to garnish

SPICED PUDDING WITH RED WINE GLAZE

This pudding is particularly suited to a winter's night, when the rich vapours will warm the soul.

The preparation of the spiced pudding can be completed in the morning, placed in the cooking moulds ready for baking, then refrigerated. The red wine glaze may also be prepared in advance then warmed at serving time.

We use 150ml (5 fl oz) aluminium moulds to bake the pudding. This size will yield 6–8 portions. If these moulds are not available a small loaf tin may be used although the pudding may not look as attractive.

Once baked the pudding must be served immediately as it is light and airy and will deflate rapidly. We would suggest having all your plates set up with the glaze and everything ready to go prior to removing the puddings from the oven.

INGREDIENTS — SERVES 6-8

100g	(3½ oz)	unsalted butter
100g	(3½ oz)	flour
2 tbsp		cocoa
2		generous pinches ground cinnamon
2		generous pinches ground ginger
250ml	(8½ fl oz)	milk
8		egg whites
6		egg yolks
50g	(1½ oz)	mixed peel, finely chopped
100g	(3½ oz)	castor sugar
		whipped cream to garnish

RED WINE GLAZE

		zest of 1 orange
100g	(3½ oz)	castor sugar
150g	(5½ oz)	red berries (raspberries, blackberries, boysenberries)
200ml	(7 fl oz)	red wine
200ml	(7 fl oz)	port
½		cinnamon stick
		juice of 1 orange
		juice of 1 lemon
1 tsp		arrowroot

METHOD: Heat the butter in a medium-sized pot. Add the flour and make a roux. Cook them together over a gentle heat for 4–5 minutes, stirring regularly. Do not brown. Remove from the heat then mix in the cocoa and the spices.

In another pot bring the milk to the boil. Beat the milk into the roux a little at a time. Return the roux to a gentle heat and continue to cook for between 30 seconds and 1 minute, beating with a wooden spoon.

Place the mixture in a clean cold bowl and allow to cool a little. Beat in 2 egg whites, a little at a time, then mix in the egg yolks one at a time. Make sure the mixture is smooth before adding the next egg yolk. Mix in the chopped mixed peel.

In a clean bowl whip the remaining 6 egg whites to a fluffy snow, adding the sugar as you go. (Start adding the sugar once the whites are half beaten.)

Using a balloon whisk, mix one-third of the snow into the spiced base, then carefully fold in the remaining snow with a large spoon. Place aside until required. Do not bang or shake the mixture or you may lose some of the air in it.

Brush all the moulds with plenty of soft butter then dust with castor sugar. Place in the refrigerator to firm up, then evenly fill each mould. Refrigerate until required for baking.

RED WINE GLAZE: Just cover the zest with water then add a teaspoon of the sugar. Cook the zest over a gentle heat until all the water has gone. Remove from the heat.

Put all the remaining ingredients except the arrowroot in a medium-sized pot and bring to the boil. Dilute the arrowroot in a little water then whisk into the red wine mixture. Lower the heat and simmer for 1 minute. Pass through a fine sieve into a clean bowl. Add the zest then cover and place in the refrigerator if the glaze is not for immediate use.

TO COOK AND SERVE: Place the puddings in a bain-marie and cook in a preheated 180°C (350°F) oven for 25–30 minutes, with the fan on.

Warm the glaze then evenly divide between six to eight rimmed soup plates. Remove the puddings from the oven and ease out of the moulds. Place on the glaze. Serve immediately with whipped cream.

CHOCOLATE SABLÉ WITH RASPBERRIES

This is our variation of a classic dessert, one that we have found very popular. The simple preparation and striking presentation make it a good option. The chocolate sablé biscuits can be eaten on their own. If possible sort out even-sized, firm raspberries.

INGREDIENTS — SERVES 6

200g	(7 oz)	unsalted butter
100g	(3½ oz)	icing sugar
		pinch of salt
2		egg yolks
215g	(7½ oz)	flour
4½ tbsp		cocoa
800g	(1¾ lb)	fresh whole raspberries
		icing sugar for dusting
		mint to garnish

COULIS

200g	(7 oz)	raspberries
300ml	(10 fl oz)	sugar syrup (see page 134)

CRÈME ANGLAISE

450ml	(15 fl oz)	milk
1		vanilla pod, split
6		egg yolks
100g	(3½ oz)	sugar

METHOD: Cut the butter into small pieces, place in a bowl and work with your fingers until soft. Sift the icing sugar then mix it into the butter along with the pinch of salt. Carefully add the egg yolks and mix well.

Sift the flour then sift the cocoa into the flour. A little at a time, mix the flour into the butter until it is all incorporated. Place on a lightly dusted work surface and knead with your hand three or four times only. Roll into a cylinder, cover in plastic wrap and store in the refrigerator for 1 hour before using.

Once rested remove from the refrigerator and allow to slightly soften. Lightly flour a flat surface and roll the pastry out to a thickness of approximately 2–3mm (½–⅛″). Using a fluted 7cm (2¾″) round pastry cutter, cut out 18 biscuits, place on a baking sheet and place in a preheated 200 °C (400 °F) oven for 5–6 minutes. Allow to cool on racks.

COULIS: Place the raspberries and sugar syrup in a liquidiser and process until smooth. Pass through a fine sieve into a clean bowl. Cover and place in the refrigerator until required.

CRÈME ANGLAISE: Place a small heavy-bottomed pot over a medium heat. Pour in the milk and add the split vanilla pod. Bring to the boil.

Place the egg yolks and sugar in a bowl and beat until the mixture turns pale yellow. Remove the vanilla pod then pour half the hot milk into the egg yolks, stirring as you go. Pour the egg mixture back into the remaining milk and place over a gentle heat. Stirring constantly, cook the mixture until it thickens enough to coat the back of the wooden spoon. Do not allow to boil.

Once cooked pass through a fine sieve into a clean bowl. Allow to cool, stirring from time to time. Cover and place in the refrigerator until required.

TO SERVE: Place one chocolate sablé in the middle of each plate, evenly arrange some raspberries on each sablé, then spoon a little of the coulis onto the berries. Add another layer of sablé, raspberries and coulis, then top with a chocolate sablé and lightly dust with icing sugar. Evenly spoon the crème anglaise around each sablé, garnish with fresh mint and serve immediately.

PAVLOVA SANDWICH WITH CARAMEL SAUCE

This dessert, which is really just a variation of the French meringue cake, was certainly named after the Russian ballerina Anna Pavlova, but there has always been much debate as to whether it was created by a New Zealand or Australian chef. It would be nice to claim it as a New Zealand recipe, but most of the evidence indicates its being created by an Australian chef to celebrate Madame Pavlova's visit to Australia in 1926.

This version of pavlova is easy to prepare and always popular. We prefer to fill the pavlova with berry fruit, such as raspberries and blueberries, but many other fruit combinations will do as well.

INGREDIENTS — SERVES 6-8

MERINGUE

4	egg whites
	pinch of salt
4 tbsp	cold water
250g (9 oz)	castor sugar
1 tsp	white wine vinegar
1 tsp	vanilla essence
4 tsp	cornflour

CARAMEL SAUCE

250g (9 oz)	castor sugar
150ml (5 fl oz)	water
250ml (8½ fl oz)	cream

FILLING

100g (3½ oz)	shelled hazelnuts
1½ tbsp	frangelico
400ml (13½ fl oz)	cream
400g (14 oz)	berry fruit

MERINGUE: Place the egg whites and salt in a perfectly clean and dry bowl. Beat until stiff. Add the cold water a little at a time then gradually add the sugar, beating constantly, until it is all in and the mixture is very stiff and stands in peaks. Fold in the vinegar, vanilla and cornflour with a metal spoon.

Lightly brush a baking tray with vegetable oil then cover with a sheet of greaseproof paper. Mark out two 12cm x 24cm (4½" x 9½") rectangles on the paper then lightly brush with vegetable oil.

Spread half the mixture within one rectangle and the remainder within the other. The top of one should be relatively smooth, as this will be the base, but the other should be covered in peaks. Place in a preheated 150°C (300°F) oven for 35 minutes, with the fan on. Once the time is up turn the oven off and allow the meringue to cool in the oven. When cool, carefully remove from tray and peel off greaseproof paper.

CARAMEL SAUCE: Place the sugar and water in a heavy pot and caramelise to a deep amber colour.

Bring the cream to just below boiling point, then carefully add to the sugar. Mix together until the toffee is dissolved. Do not boil too hard. Pass through a fine sieve into a clean bowl, cover and keep at room temperature. You may keep the sauce in the refrigerator, although it will have to be warmed before use.

FILLING: Place the hazelnuts on a baking tray and roast in a preheated 190°C (375°F) oven for 4 minutes or until they begin to brown. Allow to cool, then place in a paper bag and rub together to remove the husks. Pour onto a plate and pick out the whole nuts. Place the nuts in a food processor and blend until they are quite finely ground.

Add the frangelico to the cream and whip to a soft piping consistency. Fold in the ground hazelnuts.

TO ASSEMBLE AND SERVE: Place the meringue that will form the top of the pavlova under a hot grill and carefully colour the surface. It should be dark brown. Allow to cool.

Turn the other meringue over so that the very flat surface is facing up. Evenly spread over half the nut cream then place a layer of fruit on the cream. Spread the remaining cream over the flat side of the top meringue then sandwich them together with the dark brown surface facing up.

Place the pavlova sandwich on a serving tray and place the caramel sauce in a separate sauce boat, or dribble the sauce over the pavlova. Garnish with mint, if desired, and serve immediately.

ORANGE FLAVOURED WAFFLES
WITH APPLE COMPÔTE AND APPLE SYRUP

Waffles are always good for spur of the moment preparation.
The batter in this recipe is quite thick but very versatile, lending itself well to a variety of flavours. We use an 18cm (7") electric non-stick round waffle iron.
The non-stick element makes the cooking of the waffles very efficient. If using an uncoated iron be sure to brush with butter before putting the batter in.

INGREDIENTS — SERVES 6

APPLE COMPÔTE

5–6	medium-sized apples
	zest of 1 orange
	juice of 1 orange
2½ tbsp	castor sugar
75g (2½ oz)	sultanas

APPLE SYRUP

100ml (3½ fl oz)	clear apple concentrate
100ml (3½ fl oz)	water
100g (3½ oz)	castor sugar
1 tsp	arrowroot

WAFFLES

250g (9 oz)	flour
1 tbsp	castor sugar
	pinch of salt
3	egg yolks
1 tbsp	finely chopped orange zest
300ml (10 fl oz)	cream
1 tbsp	melted butter
3	egg whites
	icing sugar for dusting
	mint to garnish

APPLE COMPÔTE: Peel and quarter the apples. Remove the seeds then thinly slice each quarter. Place the apple, a little water, the zest, the juice and the sugar in a heavy-bottomed pot. Cover with a lid then place over a gentle heat and cook, stirring regularly, until the apple is very soft and the zest tender.

Mix in the sultanas and cook for a further 2 minutes.

Place in a clean bowl, allow to cool then cover and place in the refrigerator. The compôte will taste better if made the day before it is required.

APPLE SYRUP: Mix the apple concentrate and water together.

Place the sugar in a heavy-bottomed pot and caramelise to a light amber colour. Remove from heat and very carefully add the apple juice a little at a time until mixed in. Return to a gentle heat if necessary to melt any large lumps of toffee. Bring to the boil. Dilute the arrowroot in a little water then thicken the syrup.

Pass through a fine sieve into a clean bowl. Cover and store at room temperature.

WAFFLES: Mix the flour, sugar and salt together in a large bowl.

Place the egg yolks in a bowl with the finely chopped zest then beat until pale yellow. Add the cream and lightly mix together.

Make a well in the flour and pour in the liquid, mixing as you go. Using a wooden spoon, beat until smooth. Beat in the melted butter. Add one of the egg whites and beat until completely incorporated.

Whisk the remaining two whites until fluffy then mix as carefully as possible into the batter.

Leave to stand for 15 minutes at room temperature.

TO COOK AND SERVE: Preheat the waffle iron, then cook 18–20 waffles in four or five batches. In an electric waffle iron they will take 3–4 minutes, in a non-electric iron 2–3 minutes each side. Reheat the iron between each batch.

Turn the waffles out onto a cutting surface. Cut into portions, place three waffles on each plate and dust with icing sugar. Divide the cold compôte evenly between each plate then pour over the syrup.

Garnish with mint and serve at once.

POACHED PEACHES GRATINATED WITH MUSCAT SABAYON

There are over 2000 varieties of peaches, which are thought to have originated in China. For this dessert choose a variety with a beautiful red blush to it: once peeled, the combination of red and gold will be striking. Buy firm unblemished peaches.

We use Muscat de Beaumes de Venise from the Rhône region of France, but any good fortified dessert wine will do. To add a little crunch we serve light tuiles with the peaches. If possible use a non-stick teflon baking sheet when baking the tuiles as this will make their handling far easier.

INGREDIENTS — SERVES 6

6		medium-sized peaches
		vanilla sugar syrup (see page 134)
36		whole raspberries

TUILES

60g	(2 oz)	unsalted butter
2		egg whites
110g	(4 oz)	castor sugar
60g	(2oz)	flour
		zest of 1 orange, very finely chopped

SABAYON

75ml	(2½ fl oz)	sugar syrup (see page 134)
100ml	(3½ fl oz)	muscat
100g	(3½ oz)	castor sugar
8		egg yolks

METHOD: Cut the peaches in half then remove the stones. Bring the vanilla sugar syrup to the simmer and plunge the peaches into it. Cook them until they are soft enough to offer only little resistance to a skewer. Remember they will continue to cook for a short time after they have been removed from the syrup.

Remove the peach halves from the liquid and allow them to cool a little before carefully removing the skin. Lay each half stone-side down on a paper towel to cool completely. Cover then place in the refrigerator until required.

This part of preparation may be completed the day or morning before.

TUILES: Place all the ingredients except the orange zest in a bowl or food processor and mix until very smooth. Mix in the zest.

Liberally brush a baking tray with butter then dust with flour. Tap off excess flour. Cook the tuiles in batches of four to six. Mark out 10cm (4") circles in the flour on the tray then thinly spread the batter to the marked size.

Cook in a preheated 190°C (375°F) oven for 3–5 minutes until dark brown round the edges and golden in the centre. Remove from the oven and while still hot use a flexible palette knife to remove the tuiles from the tray. Fold them in half. When cool store them in an airtight container until needed.

SABAYON AND TO SERVE: Heat a grill or salamander to very hot. Place two halves of peach in the middle of a flat plate. Arrange three berries either side of the fruit.

Warm the muscat a little then mix in the sugar. Stir together for a few seconds then pour into a sabayon basin or round bowl. Add the egg yolks and sugar syrup then place over a gentle heat and whisk until the mixture has doubled in quantity and the whisk leaves tracks.

Evenly spoon the sabayon around and over the peaches. Place the plate under the grill immediately, to set the sabayon before the air begins to escape, and allow to brown. Take care as the sabayon will colour rapidly.

Remove the plate from the heat then place a tuile at the top and bottom of the plate. Serve while the sabayon is still warm.

LEMON VERBENA CAKE WITH TEQUILA AND LIME SYRUP

Although this is a slightly heavier cake, more like a pudding, it is very easy to eat because of the lemony flavour. Lemon verbena is a native of Chile and has the flavour of lemon without the acidity. It is available fresh or dried. You may leave the tequila out if you prefer and you may also serve this cake with lemon syrup.

INGREDIENTS — SERVES 12

410g	(14½ oz)	flour
1 tsp		salt
2 tsp		baking powder
200ml	(7 fl oz)	vegetable oil
470g	(16½ fl oz)	sugar
3		eggs
		zest of 1 lemon, finely chopped
260ml	(9 fl oz)	milk
2 tbsp		fresh lemon verbena, finely chopped
		icing sugar for dusting
		mint to garnish
		sablé biscuits to garnish (see page 137)

SYRUP

		zest of 2 limes
150g	(5½ oz)	castor sugar
75ml	(2½ fl oz)	orange juice
100ml	(3½ fl oz)	lime juice
100ml	(3½ fl oz)	tequila
1 tsp		arrowroot

METHOD: Sift together the flour, salt and baking powder. In a separate bowl combine the sugar and oil well. Mix in the eggs and zest. Add half the milk then half the flour to the egg mixture. Mix together until well combined. Finally stir in the remaining milk and flour then add the lemon verbena.

Butter then flour a 24cm (9½″) spring-form cake tin then pour in the batter. Bake in a preheated 170°C (325°F) oven for 30 minutes, with the fan on. Reduce the oven to 100°C (210°F) then continue to bake for a further 45 minutes with the fan off.

Check the cake is cooked by inserting a toothpick into the centre. It should come out clean. Remove from the oven and allow to cool, then remove from the tin and place on a cake rack to cool completely.

SYRUP: Cover the zest in water, add a good pinch of the sugar then cook until the zest is tender. Remove any excess cooking water.

Combine the rest of the sugar, the juice and the tequila in a pot then bring to the boil. Thicken with arrowroot diluted in water. Pass the syrup through a fine sieve onto the cooked zest, mix together then place the syrup in a clean bowl.

Cover with plastic wrap and place in the refrigerator.

TO SERVE: Cut a wedge of cake then dust the top with icing sugar. Place the cake in the middle of a plate and spoon on a pool of cold syrup. Garnish with a sprig of mint and a sablé biscuit cut into the shape of a cactus.

VARIATION: You may also fill the cake with lemon curd. Cut the cake in half and brush both sides with tequila and syrup then spread one side with cold curd. Garnish as above.

KIWIFRUIT CRÊPE SOUFFLÉ

One of Europe's oldest and most basic foods, rich in tradition, the pancake has been elevated to the greatest heights of haute cuisine. Such renowned dishes as crêpe suzette have helped make this simple dish popular throughout the world.

Kiwifruit was first planted in New Zealand in 1906, but it is a native of China. It was named after the national bird of New Zealand, the kiwi, most likely because the colour and shape of the fruit resembles the bird. Kiwifruit is an excellent source of vitamin C and should be eaten when slightly soft.

INGREDIENTS — SERVES 6-8

100g (3½ oz)	flour
250ml (8½ fl oz)	milk
	pinch of salt
1 tbsp	castor sugar
2	large eggs
1	egg yolk
	clarified butter for batter
	clarified butter to sauté

SOUFFLÉ

30g (1 oz)	butter
50g (1½ oz)	flour
250ml (8½ fl oz)	milk
	zest of 1 lemon, finely chopped
2	egg yolks
2 tsp	lemon juice
3-4	egg whites
100g (3½ oz)	castor sugar

GARNISH

	icing sugar for dusting
4	medium-sized kiwifruit

METHOD: Sift the flour into a bowl. Whisk in the milk, salt and sugar. Beat in the eggs and yolk then melt a knob of clarified butter and add it to the batter.

Allow the batter to stand at room temperature for 30 minutes. Beat regularly to make sure the flour doesn't settle to the bottom of the bowl.

Melt a little clarified butter in a small pan then pour off the excess. Tilt the pan a little and while the pan is still hot pour in a small ladle of batter, rolling the pan as you pour to spread the batter thinly over the bottom of the pan. This must be done quite quickly, before the batter sets. Return the pan to a medium heat and brown the pancake. Do not over brown as the pancakes will be baked later on. Toss or turn the pancakes with a palette knife and brown on the other side. Once cooked lay the pancakes over the base of an upturned bowl. Continue to cook the batter until you have 12-16 crêpes.

SOUFFLÉ: Make a roux with the butter and flour, and cook for 2 minutes, being careful not to let it brown. Beat the milk into the roux a little at a time. Mix in the zest and bring to the boil. Remove the roux from the heat, allow to cool a little then beat in the egg yolks and lemon juice.

Half whisk the egg whites then, adding the sugar as you go, whisk to a stiff snow. Beat a quarter of the whites into the roux base then carefully fold in the remaining whites. Place in the refrigerator until required.

SETTING UP: Place 12 crêpes on one large or two small baking trays. If possible line the trays with non-stick teflon sheets. Peel the kiwifruit then cut in half lengthways. Thinly slice, then divide evenly on half of each crêpe. Spread the soufflé mix over the kiwifruit about 1.5cm (½″) thick and fold the other half of the crêpe over. Lightly dust with icing sugar then place in a pre-heated 180°C (350°F) for 10-15 minutes.

TO SERVE: Warm the plates and garnish each with sliced kiwifruit.

Once cooked, place two crêpes on each plate and serve immediately. An extra pair of hands at serving time will ensure the crêpes do not deflate too much before they reach the table.

A little kiwifruit purée served separately is a nice accompaniment to the crêpe soufflé.

LEMON MERINGUE PIE

This pie should have a strong but sweet lemon flavour. The pastry case should be well browned and crumbly and the meringue topping nicely caramelised.

We usually prepare the case and curd in the morning then assemble the pie and keep it covered in a cool place (not the refrigerator). The meringue topping is prepared and placed on top within an hour of serving to avoid the meringue softening and sliding off the pie once it is cut.

Egg whites increase in volume when whipped because they contain a high 11 percent protein. This protein forms tiny filaments that stretch on beating, incorporating air in tiny bubbles and enabling the whites to expand up to seven times their original volume. The whites must be fresh with absolutely no yolk present and the bowl and whisk must be scrupulously clean and dry. Add 3 teaspoons of the castor sugar once the whites are half beaten to reduce the chance of overbeating.

INGREDIENTS — SERVES 6-8

250g (9 oz)	pâte sablée (see page 137)

LEMON FILLING

3	medium-sized lemons
250ml (8½ fl oz)	sugar syrup (see page 134)
½	vanilla pod, split

LEMON CURD

200g (7 oz)	castor sugar
	zest of 2 lemons, grated
300ml (10 fl oz)	water
4½ tbsp	cornflour
30g (1 oz)	unsalted butter
	juice of 3 lemons
3	egg yolks

MERINGUE

3	egg whites
100g (3½ oz)	castor sugar

METHOD: Prepare the pâte sablée according to the instructions on page 137. Roll it to 2mm ($^1/_{12}$") thick, being careful not to over handle.

Place a 20cm (8") flan ring on a baking sheet then line it with the pastry. Line the pastry with a circle of greaseproof paper and fill with beans or rice. Rest pastry in the refrigerator for 15 minutes, then bake in a preheated 190°C (375°F) oven for 15-18 minutes or until well browned around the top edge.

Remove the paper and beans or rice and allow the case to cool in the ring out of the refrigerator.

LEMON FILLING: Slice each lemon (with the skin on) very finely into rings. Remove all pips then place in a heat-proof container and pour boiling water over the slices. Leave to steep for 2½-3 hours.

Rinse each slice in cold water then place in a large flat pan. Just cover with sugar syrup, add the split vanilla pod then gently simmer until the lemon is translucent.

Place the cooked slices in a stainless-steel bowl, cover with the cooking liquid and allow to completely cool.

LEMON CURD: Add the sugar and grated zest to the water then boil over a high heat until the sugar has dissolved. Continue to boil for 1 minute. Dilute the cornflour in a little water then whisk into the sugar and water. Boil for 1 minute.

Remove from the heat and add the butter and lemon juice. Beat in the yolks one at a time. Return to a gentle heat and cook, stirring constantly, until the mixture thickens a little. Keep warm.

TO COOK AND SERVE: Pat the lemon slices dry then evenly cover the bottom of the baked flan case with a layer of lemon, just overlapping each slice. Pour in the curd while it is still hot and spread evenly. Allow to set then remove the flan ring.

To make the meringue, beat the egg whites until they begin to stiffen then sprinkle in a handful of the castor sugar. Continue to beat until the whites are at a stiff peak. Sprinkle on the remaining sugar and carefully mix it in.

Evenly spoon or pipe the snow onto the pie. Place on a baking tray in a preheated 230-250°C (450-500°F) oven and bake for a couple of minutes, until the meringue is well browned.

Serve whole on an elegant cake dish or cut it into wedges with a sharp knife. Serve at room temperature.

RHUBARB MOUSSE OVER HONEY CRÈME ANGLAISE

Fresh, crisp rhubarb combined with the natural creamy sweetness of honey crème anglaise provides a classic example of tasty simplicity.

Rhubarb is a native of China, where it has been used as a medicine for the past 5000 years.

For this dessert use fresh rhubarb that is as red as possible, to make the mousse a lovely pastel pink. We use runny honey in the crème anglaise as it is easier to handle. We keep the liquid that the rhubarb has been cooked in then reduce it over heat to a concentrated syrup. It is then used to add flavour and eye appeal.

INGREDIENTS — SERVES 6

400g	(14 oz)	fresh rhubarb
900ml	(30 fl oz)	water
250g	(9 oz)	castor sugar
		juice of 2 oranges
		juice of 1 lemon
3		gelatine leaves
200ml	(7 fl oz)	cream
1		egg white
18 pieces		cooked rhubarb to garnish
30		chocolate cigars to garnish (see page 130)

CRÈME ANGLAISE

450ml	(15 fl oz)	milk
6		egg yolks
50g	(1½ oz)	sugar
3 tbsp		runny honey

METHOD: Wash the rhubarb and cut it into 2.5cm (1″) lengths. Place in a medium-sized heavy-bottomed pot. Add the water, sugar and all the fruit juice. Place over a medium to high heat and cook until the rhubarb is quite soft.

Remove the rhubarb from the cooking liquid with a slotted spoon or sieve, Place in a food processor and blend until very smooth. While still hot, place in a clean bowl.

Soak the gelatine leaves in cold water then add to the hot rhubarb purée. Stir until all the gelatine has dissolved. If necessary return to a gentle heat and stir.

Push the purée through a fine sieve into a clean bowl. Cool over ice, stirring from time to time to ensure even cooling.

Lightly whip the cream then, in a separate bowl, beat the egg white to a soft, fluffy consistency.

Allow the purée to set to the consistency of unbeaten egg white, then evenly mix in the whipped cream. Finally, fold in the whisked egg white carefully — don't over mix or the light and airy effect will be lost.

Divide the mousse evenly between six 100ml (3½ fl oz) moulds and place them in the refrigerator for at least 1½ hours.

CRÈME ANGLAISE: Place a small heavy-bottomed pot over a medium heat. Pour in the milk and bring to the boil. Lower the heat. Place the egg yolks, sugar and honey in a bowl and beat until the mixture turns a pale yellow. Pour in half the hot milk and mix together.

Pour the egg mixture into the remaining milk and place over a gentle heat. Stirring constantly with a wooden spoon, cook the mixture until it thickens enough to coat the back of the spoon. Do not allow it to boil. Pass through a fine sieve into a clean bowl. Allow to cool, stirring from time to time, then cover with plastic wrap and put aside. Keep at room temperature.

TO SERVE: Unmould the mousses onto chilled plates by quickly dipping the containers in warm water then shaking them out. Evenly divide the crème anglaise between each plate and spread it out to the edge of the plate. Spoon the reduced cooling liquid over each mousse, allowing it to run into the crème anglaise a little.

Place three pieces of poached rhubarb and five chocolate cigars around each plate. Serve at room temperature.

PEARS CARAMELISED IN HONEY
WITH VANILLA ICE CREAM AND SABAYON

In this dessert we use the base vanilla ice cream recipe. The ice cream may be prepared in advance, and to help serve the dish quickly I would recommend making the quenelles of ice cream ahead of time also. Simply form and place on a chilled tray, cover and leave in the freezer.

As with most of our desserts in which pears feature, choose firm, unblemished, even-sized fruit with a good pear shape. Winter Cole, Comice and Packham are all good varieties for this dessert.

You may also cook the pears several hours in advance and reheat when required.

INGREDIENTS — SERVES 6

4½	ripe but firm medium-sized pears
1 tbsp	clarified butter
6 tbsp	runny honey
	vanilla ice cream (see page 132)
	mint to garnish

SABAYON

5	egg yolks
100ml (3½ fl oz)	sugar syrup (see page 134)
60ml (2 fl oz)	Poire William liqueur

METHOD: Peel the pears and cut in half. Cut into quarters then carefully remove the seeds and core. Using a small sharp knife make shallow criss-cross incisions on the outside of each quarter.

Cook the pears in batches of six, so that you can control the cooking process and prevent the pears from stewing as a result of excess heat loss. In a small sauté pan or shallow pot, melt one-third of the clarified butter over a high heat. Place six of the pear wedges in the hot pan and quickly brown on all sides. Remove from the heat and turn the pears onto their criss-cross bases. Add one-third of the honey to the pot. Place over a low-medium heat and cook until the honey is a light brown. Turn the pears and continue to cook until they are just slightly firm. The honey should be quite a dark brown but at no time smell burnt.

Place the cooked pears on a tray suitable for reheating then continue with the next two batches. You will need to clean the pan between each batch.

Store the cooked pears at room temperature, covered with plastic wrap.

Form 12 quenelles by taking a tablespoon of the frozen ice cream, then dipping a second tablespoon in cold water and scooping the ice cream from one spoon to the other, forming a three-sided barrel shape. Place on a well-chilled tray and freeze.

When doing this keep everything well chilled so the ice cream doesn't melt. Form in batches if necessary.

SABAYON AND TO SERVE: Place the pears in a 180 °C (350 °F) oven to warm through.

Place the sabayon ingredients in a bowl over a pot of simmering water. Using a balloon whisk beat the mixture until it is light and fluffy and doubled in quantity. Remove from the heat.

Arrange three warm pieces of pear and two ice cream quenelles tidily on each of six flat plates.

Divide the sabayon evenly between the plates, garnish with mint and serve immediately.

LIME AND BUTTERMILK TARTE WITH LEMON AND WINE CREAM

Originally buttermilk was the sour milk by-product of butter making, but nowadays it is made from skimmed milk thickened with a culture. Buttermilk is used in baking and as a sour milk drink.
The lime is of Indian origin and is closely related to the lemon. The combination of the two in this recipe results in a tangy yet sweet tarte. We use a 26cm (10½") flan ring for the pastry case, but a suitable pie dish will do.

INGREDIENTS — SERVES 8–10

500–600g (18–21 oz)	pâte sablée (see page 137)
10	eggs
450g (1 lb)	castor sugar
4½ tbsp	flour
850ml (1¾ US pints)	buttermilk
135g (5 oz)	butter
	juice of 3 limes
	zest of 3 limes, finely chopped
	cinnamon for dusting
	mint to garnish

LEMON AND WINE CREAM

100g (3½ oz)	castor sugar
60ml (2 fl oz)	sweet or fruit white wine
600ml (20 fl oz)	cream
	juice of 4 lemons
3	walnuts, finely chopped

METHOD: Lightly flour a flat surface then roll out the pastry to approximately 4mm (⅙"). Place the flan ring on a baking tray and line it with the pastry. Work quickly as the pastry will become very difficult to work with if it becomes too warm. Rest the lined flan ring in the refrigerator for 15 minutes or until it is firm.

Line the inside of the pastry case with greaseproof paper then fill with beans or rice. Bake blind in a preheated 175–180°C (330–350°F) oven for approximately 20 minutes. Allow to cool slightly, then carefully remove the beans or rice. While the case is still warm remove the paper lining. Leave the case in the flan ring and allow to cool to room temperature. Thoroughly brush the pastry case with one of the eggs, beaten. Return the case to the oven and bake for 1–2 minutes, until the egg has set. Repeat this process, then allow the case to cool, leaving the ring on and the baking tray in place.

Beat the rest of the eggs with the sugar until light and creamy. Sift the flour into the egg mixture and combine. Add the buttermilk and mix together thoroughly.

Melt the butter with the lime juice and zest then add to the egg and buttermilk filling. Carefully pour into the prepared case, watching out for leaks. If there are any, plug them with leftover pastry trimmings. Dust the top of the tarte with cinnamon then place in a 160°C (310°F) oven for 45–50 minutes, with the fan on.

Allow the tarte to cool to room temperature on the tray. Run a sharp knife around the inside of the ring, trimming off excess pastry, then remove the ring. Store in a cool place, but not in the refrigerator.

LEMON AND WINE CREAM: Dissolve the sugar in the wine. Place the cream in a separate bowl and whisk lightly. Add the lemon juice and the wine mixture to the cream a little at a time, mixing well as the cream thickens. Do not over beat. Carefully mix in the finely chopped walnuts.

Cover with plastic wrap and refrigerate for 2 hours before serving.

TO SERVE: Slice the tarte into wedges then place each slice on a serving plate. Spoon on a good-sized serving of the cream mixture, garnish with mint then serve.

BOILED FRUIT PUDDINGS WITH SPICED PRUNES AND AMARETTO CRÈME ANGLAISE

This is a light steamed pudding, and at Huka Lodge we cook the entire quantity in one large pudding basin. However, at home I use five 450ml (15 fl oz) fruit tins. Simply eat the contents of the tin for breakfast, take the lid off, peel off the label and wash the can. The modern fruit tin is lined to prevent corrosion but, to be safe, make sure the tins are kept completely dry in storage. Use them then discard them.

Once cooked, the puddings are easily removed from each tin and form handy cylinders that can be sliced into perfect medallions or cut in half. The puddings will freeze very well if encased in plastic wrap. They can be served cold or warm.

The spiced prunes can be substituted by poached or bottled apricots, plums, figs or feijoas, and the amaretto may be omitted from the crème anglaise. The fruit in the puddings may be substituted by nuts or chopped chocolate couverture.

If you use prunes they will have to be soaked overnight. The crème anglaise may also be prepared the day before, covered and kept in the refrigerator.

INGREDIENTS — SERVES 8–10

3–4		pitted prunes per serving
100g	(3½ oz)	castor sugar
¼ tsp		ground cloves
½ tsp		ground ginger
½ tsp		ground cinnamon
¼ tsp		freshly grated nutmeg
600ml	(20 fl oz)	water
500ml	(17 fl oz)	crème anglaise (see page 98)
2 tbsp		amaretto
		mint to garnish

PUDDINGS

300g	(10½ oz)	wholemeal flour
150g	(5½ oz)	flour
1 tsp		mixed spice
2 tsp		baking soda
450ml	(15 fl oz)	milk
240ml	(8 fl oz)	golden syrup
50g	(1½ oz)	currants
50g	(1½ oz)	dried figs, chopped
50g	(1½ oz)	dried apricots, chopped

METHOD: Place the prunes in a large bowl.

Put the sugar, spices and water in a pot then gently warm over a medium heat, stirring constantly, until the sugar has dissolved. Pour the warm liquid over the prunes, cover and place in the refrigerator overnight.

Make the crème anglaise according to the instructions on page 98, adding the amaretto to the egg yolks. Cover and store in the refrigerator.

PUDDINGS: Bring a large pot, half full of water, to the boil.

Meanwhile, place all the flour, spice and baking soda in a large bowl. Make a well in the flour then pour in the milk and golden syrup. Slowly incorporate the liquid then mix together well. Stir in all the dried fruit.

Brush each tin liberally with butter then half fill with pudding mixture. Cover the tops with buttered aluminium foil then place each tin carefully into the pot of boiling water. The water should come halfway up the side of the tins. You will need to top the water up two or three times while the puddings are cooking: be sure to use hot water. Cook the puddings for 1 hour at a steady simmer.

To check if the puddings are cooked, lift one tin out and look under the aluminium foil. If the mixture is still sticky continue cooking. Once they are cooked, slip a small knife around the edge then shake the puddings out onto a cake rack to cool.

TO SERVE: If you are serving the puddings hot you will need to set up the plates in advance. Spoon some crème anglaise onto each plate then arrange a small pile of spiced prunes with a sprig of mint on top.

Once the puddings are cooked, remove from the tins, cool slightly then, with a sharp or electric knife, slice the puddings into medallions or in half and arrange tidily on each plate. Serve while still warm.

NUT SPONGE AND MULLED WINE JELLY TRIFLE WITH ZABAGLIONE

Trifle has always been a treat, especially enjoyed by children. In the past trifles have been multi-coloured creations of jelly, sponge and custards with an abundance of candy decoration. This is a more 'grown-up' version, easy to prepare and just as tasty, with a combination of fruits, wine and nutty sponge, capped off with a rich, creamy zabaglione. If possible present this trifle in a glass bowl with a capacity of about 3.5 litres (7½ US pints).

SPONGE: Prepare and bake the sponge according to the plain sponge recipe on page 136, folding in the ground nuts after the flour and cornflour.

SHERRY JELLY: Mix the sherry and sugar syrup together then warm over a gentle heat.

Soak the gelatine leaves in cold water, squeeze out excess water then add to the warm liquid and stir until completely dissolved. Pass through a fine sieve into a clean bowl. Allow to cool to room temperature, but do not allow to set.

MULLED WINE JELLY: Place all the mulled wine jelly ingredients except the gelatine leaves in a pot and bring to the boil. Skim off impurities as they rise to the surface. Lower the heat and gently simmer for 2 minutes.

Soak the gelatine leaves in cold water, squeeze out excess water then add to the mulled wine and stir until completely dissolved. Pass through a fine sieve into a clean bowl. Allow to cool to room temperature, but do not allow to set.

TO ASSEMBLE: Slice the sponge horizontally into three even pieces. Place one slice in the bottom of the bowl then drench with one-third of the sherry jelly mixture. Refrigerate to set the jelly.

Once the jelly is set, arrange half the prepared fruit and half the orange segments on the soaked sponge. Pour half the mulled wine jelly mixture over the fruit, making sure the jelly is not at all hot. Return to the refrigerator to allow jelly to set.

Once set, place the second piece of sponge on top of the jelly and soak with half the remaining sherry jelly liquid. Return to the refrigerator to set.

Once set, spread the remaining berries and orange segments on the second layer of sponge then pour over the remaining mulled wine jelly mixture. Allow to set in the refrigerator.

Finally, place the remaining piece of sponge on top and soak with the remaining sherry jelly liquid. Cover with plastic wrap and refrigerate.

ZABAGLIONE: Place the egg yolks, sugar and salt in a large stainless-steel bowl. Beat together. Mix in the sherry and marsala. Place over a pot of simmering water and beat constantly with a whisk, until the mixture is thick and tripled in volume. The eggs must be cooked enough that the sabayon is past ribbon stage, or the finished cream will be too runny.

Remove from the heat and place over a larger bowl of ice. Continue to whisk until the mixture is completely cold.

Whip the cream to a light piping consistency then fold it into the sabayon. Evenly spread the zabaglione over the top of the chilled and set trifle.

TO SERVE: Garnish the trifle with mint, fresh fruit and praline, if desired, and serve in the bowl.

INGREDIENTS — SERVES 10-12
SPONGE

		plain sponge mixture (see page 136)
100g	(3½ oz)	shelled hazelnuts, roasted and ground
100g	(3½ oz)	shelled almonds, roasted and ground

SHERRY JELLY

375ml	(12½ fl oz)	medium sherry
325ml	(11 fl oz)	sugar syrup (see page 134)
6		gelatine leaves

MULLED WINE JELLY

200g	(7 oz)	mixed red berries
300ml	(10 fl oz)	red wine
300ml	(10 fl oz)	ruby port
150g	(5½ oz)	castor sugar
		zest of 1 orange
		juice of 1 orange
½		cinnamon stick
2		cloves
6-7		gelatine leaves

FRUIT FILLING

600g	(1¼ lb)	mixed red berries (strawberries, raspberries, blackberries, blueberries)
4		large oranges, in segments

ZABAGLIONE

6		egg yolks
80g	(3 oz)	castor sugar
		pinch of salt
100ml	(3½ fl oz)	medium sherry
50ml	(1½ fl oz)	marsala
300ml	(10 fl oz)	cream

GARNISH

	mint
	fresh fruit
	ground praline (see page 33)

STOLLEN

Stollen has been baked for generations and is one of many European Christmas cakes developed by Christians to celebrate the winter solstice.

Although stollen has a traditional shape, it may also be prepared in a cake tin or as a loaf. At Huka Lodge we serve our variation of stollen as a 'sweet bread'. It is lovely with coffee or as a sweet breakfast bread. It may also be toasted. If the loaf is not to be consumed within a day or two it may be frozen. If you plan to freeze do not brush the stollen with butter and dust with icing sugar until you are ready to serve it.

This recipe yields approximately 2.4 kg (5½ lbs) of raw dough for the production of two large loaves or three small loaves. It is just as easy to prepare a large amount and freeze some as it is to prepare a small amount.

METHOD: Place the flour, fruit, almonds, salt and sugar in an electric mixer. Dissolve the yeast in the warm milk. Crack the eggs into a bowl. With the mixing machine on slow pour in the milk and yeast followed by all the eggs. Beat the mixture until the ingredients are well incorporated. Increase the speed and add the cubed butter to the dough a little at a time.

Place the dough on a lightly floured flat surface and briefly knead into a ball. Place in a large bowl, cover with a clean cloth and prove in a warm place for 30 minutes.

Turn the dough out onto a floured surface and cut into two or three even-sized pieces. Roll each piece into a ball then form into two loaves approximately 35cm (14") long or three loaves 30cm (12") long. Using a rolling pin roll the centre of each loaf so they are thicker down both sides with a 'valley' down the middle. Round off each end. Lightly brush the inside with rum then sprinkle over a little cinnamon. Finally fold over lengthways, bringing one side three-quarters of the way up the other.

Place the loaves on a baking tray and prove in a warm place, covered, for 30–40 minutes or until doubled in size.

Bake in a preheated 190 °C (375 °F) oven for 40–45 minutes, with the fan on. While still warm brush with melted butter then liberally dust with icing sugar. Cool.

Store in an airtight container or enjoy while still warm with coffee.

INGREDIENTS — MAKES 2–3

1kg	(2¼ lbs)	flour
100g	(3½ oz)	dried apricots, finely chopped
100g	(3½ oz)	sultanas
100g	(3½ oz)	mixed peel
200g	(7 oz)	blanched almonds, chopped
2½ tsp		salt
90g	(3 oz)	castor sugar
80g	(3 oz)	fresh yeast
200ml	(7 fl oz)	warm milk
5–6		eggs
260g	(9 oz)	unsalted butter, cubed
		rum for brushing
		ground cinnamon for dusting
		melted butter for brushing
		icing sugar for dusting

SPICY FRUIT LOAVES

This type of loaf can be served warm with cream, cold with butter or even toasted. I find these loaves nice to eat at any time from breakfast to supper.

The recipes are much the same as far as method is concerned, they just have different flavourings. You may have your own favourite fruits and spices and both these recipes are very adaptable.

The quantities given make two approximately 900g (2 lb) loaves using a standard loaf tin or a 1.4 litre (3 US pint) Le Creuset terrine mould. Both recipes may safely be halved and the loaves freeze well.

DRIED FRUIT LOAF

INGREDIENTS — MAKES 2

800g	(1¾ lb)	mixed dried fruit
340g	(12 oz)	castor sugar
350ml	(12 fl oz)	water
100g	(3½ oz)	butter
500g	(17 oz)	flour
2½ tbsp		baking powder
2 tsp		ground nutmeg
2 tbsp		ground ginger
2 tbsp		ground cinnamon
3-4		eggs

METHOD: Roughly chop the dried fruit and place in a large pot with the sugar, water and butter. Bring to the boil then remove from the heat and cool to room temperature.

Place the flour, baking powder and spices in a large bowl. Make a well in the flour then mix in the fruit and liquid. Mix in 3 eggs then, if the mixture is still too dry, add the fourth egg.

Line two loaf tins with greaseproof paper then divide the mixture evenly between them and smooth the top. Place in a preheated 190°C (375°F) oven for 1 hour or until a skewer inserted into the middle comes out clean.

Once cooked allow to cool in the tin then remove and store in an airtight container or freeze in convenient-sized pieces.

DATE AND WALNUT LOAF

INGREDIENTS — MAKES 2

400g	(14 oz)	dried dates
350ml	(12 fl oz)	milk
300g	(10½ oz)	castor sugar
100g	(3½ oz)	unsalted butter
300g	(10½ oz)	shelled walnuts
500g	(17 oz)	flour
2 tbsp		baking powder
2 tsp		ground nutmeg
2 tbsp		ground cinnamon
3-4		eggs

METHOD: Roughly chop the dates and place in a large pot with the milk, sugar and butter. Bring to the boil then simmer until the butter has melted.

Roughly chop the walnuts. Place the flour, baking powder and spices in a large bowl, mix in the walnuts then add the dates and liquid and the eggs.

Line two loaf tins with greaseproof paper then divide the mixture evenly between them and smooth the top. Place in a preheated 190°C (375°F) oven for 1 hour or until a skewer inserted into the middle comes out clean.

Allow to cool in the tin and store in an airtight container or freeze.

MUFFINS

At Huka Lodge we serve a great variety of muffins, usually at breakfast but sometimes instead of dessert after a light lunch. Muffins can be sweet, fruity, full of bran for the healthy eater or served warm with runny honey and lots of butter.

PEAR MUFFINS

METHOD: Place the flour, bran flakes, cinnamon, baking powder, ginger and cloves in a large bowl and thoroughly mix together.

Put the butter, golden syrup, brown sugar and milk in a pot. Place over a gentle heat and warm until the butter melts, stirring constantly.

Peel the pears then coarsely grate into a bowl. Add the pear flesh and orange zest to the liquid ingredients then add all the liquid ingredients to the flour mixture. Do not over mix. Add the beaten egg. Rest the mixture for 15 minutes at room temperature. Using a deep 12 muffin tray, non-stick if possible, evenly divide the muffin mixture. Place in a preheated 190 °C (375 °F) oven and bake for 25–30 minutes, with the fan on.

Once baked, cool a little then remove from the tray onto a cake rack. Serve warm with butter and honey or store in an airtight container. Pear muffins freeze well.

INGREDIENTS — MAKES 12

325g	(11½ oz)	flour
70g	(2½ oz)	bran flakes
1 tsp		ground cinnamon
1½ tbsp		baking powder
½ tsp		ground ginger
½ tsp		ground cloves
45g	(1½ oz)	unsalted butter
3 tbsp		golden syrup
100g	(3½ oz)	brown sugar
320ml	(11 fl oz)	milk
2		medium-sized pears
		zest of ½ orange, chopped
1		egg, beaten

DATE MUFFINS

METHOD: Place the flour, bran flakes, castor sugar, baking powder, ginger and dates in a large bowl and thoroughly mix together.

Melt the butter in the milk over a gentle heat, stirring regularly. Beat the eggs. Add the liquid ingredients to the flour mixture and stir together. Do not over mix.

Allow the mixture to stand for 15 minutes at room temperature. Using a deep 12 muffin tray, non-stick if possible, evenly divide the muffin mixture. Place in a preheated 190 °C (375 °F) oven and bake for 25–30 minutes, with the fan on.

Once baked, cool a little then remove from the tray onto a cake rack. Store in an airtight container.

INGREDIENTS — MAKES 12

325g	(11½ oz)	flour
70g	(2½ oz)	bran flakes
190g	(6½ oz)	castor sugar
1½ tbsp		baking powder
1 tbsp		ground ginger
300g	(10½ oz)	dried dates, chopped
100g	(3½ oz)	unsalted butter
350ml	(12 fl oz)	milk
3		eggs

BANANA MUFFINS

INGREDIENTS — MAKES 12

280g	(10 oz)	flour
90g	(3 oz)	castor sugar
1½ tbsp		baking powder
4		ripe bananas
3½ tbsp		milk
2		eggs
75ml	(2½ fl oz)	walnut or sunflower oil
		zest of 1 lemon, roughly chopped
75g	(2½ oz)	sultanas

METHOD: Place the flour, sugar and baking powder in a large bowl. Mash the bananas with the milk, eggs and oil, then add the zest and sultanas. Carefully mix the banana mixture into the flour. Do not over mix or the texture of the muffins will be spoiled.

Allow the mixture to stand at room temperature for 15 minutes. Using a deep 12 muffin tray, non-stick if possible, evenly divide the muffin mixture. Place in a preheated 190°C (375°F) oven and bake for 25–30 minutes, with the fan on.

Once baked, cool a little then remove from the tray onto a cake rack. Store in an airtight container or freeze and reheat in a gentle oven when required.

PRUNE AND PECAN MUFFINS

INGREDIENTS — MAKES 12

TOPPING

3 tbsp		flour
2 tbsp		brown sugar
½ tsp		mixed spice
1 tbsp		unsalted butter

MUFFINS

1		egg
2 tbsp		unsalted butter, melted
250ml	(8½ fl oz)	plain unsweetened yoghurt
½ tsp		mixed spice
2 tsp		baking powder
85g	(3 oz)	castor sugar
75g	(2½ oz)	flour
75g	(2½ oz)	chopped pecans

PRUNE FILLING

125ml	(4 fl oz)	puréed prunes
1 tbsp		unsalted butter, melted
1 tbsp		castor sugar
½ tsp		ground cinnamon

TOPPING: Mix all the ingredients together, roll into a ball then place in the refrigerator to firm up.

PRUNE FILLING: Mix all the filling ingredients together then place aside until required.

MUFFINS: Mix the egg, melted butter, yoghurt and mixed spice together well in a large bowl. Add the baking powder, sugar and flour and carefully combine with the yoghurt mixture. Do not over mix. Finally, carefully fold in the chopped pecans.

Divide half the muffin mixture evenly over a 12-muffin tray. Place a small spoonful of prune filling in the middle of each half full mould, then top up each with the remaining muffin mixture. Carefully grate the firmed topping over each muffin.

Place in a preheated 200°C (400°F) oven and bake for 15–20 minutes, with the fan on. Once baked, remove from the oven, allow to cool a little then remove from the muffin tray and cool on a cake rack.

FRUIT SELECTION

COLOUR: A good variety of fresh, fruity colours is always effective.

HEIGHT: Try to have a central high area in the presentation or, as in the photograph, a high area at the top with everything else flowing down from there.

TEXTURE: Mix smooth-textured fruit with crunchy fruit.

ACIDITY AND SWEETNESS: Make sure you have a balance of sweet fruits, such as pawpaw and melon, and acid fruits, such as citrus fruits and kiwifruit.

FRESHNESS: The fruit must look and be fresh. Prepare the selection just before serving.

Fruit, nature's dessert, is a perfect finish to any meal at any time of day or night. The varieties and combinations are endless.

The fruit we use varies according to the season. Often we serve our fruit selections with a fresh fruit coulis (see page 98) or citrus syrup (page 92), but sometimes we serve them with a tuile basket (page 128) or, as in this case, a chocolate wafer (page 131).

Keep the opposite points in mind when serving a fruit selection.

TUILE BASKETS

INGREDIENTS — MAKES 6

75g (2½ oz)	castor sugar
	pinch of ground cinnamon
1	egg
3 tbsp	flour
1 tbsp	cream
1 tsp	finely chopped almonds

METHOD: Cream together the sugar, cinnamon and egg using a wooden spoon. Try not to froth the mixture or beat in air bubbles. Stir in the flour. Cover and rest in the refrigerator for 1 hour. Once rested, mix in the cream. The consistency should be that of a batter.

Brush a baking tray with plenty of butter then dust thoroughly with flour. With a 10cm (4″) plain cutter mark out six evenly spaced circles. Spread the batter thinly within each circle. Sprinkle on the finely chopped almonds.

Set out six brioche or similar moulds on the bench top ready to shape tuiles. Bake the tuiles in a 180°C (350°F) oven for 2-3 minutes. Great care must be taken at this stage. The tuiles must be just set with very little or no colour, and very floppy but not overly sticky.

Now you must work quickly before the baking tray and tuiles cool. Slide a palette knife under each disc and lift it off the baking tray. Drop into the mould and press into shape with your fingertips. If you find the last couple of tuiles are too set and won't bend, return them to the oven for 30 seconds to heat up again, then press them into shape.

Return the tuiles to the oven and continue to bake until evenly browned, for approximately 2 minutes.

Allow to cool, then remove from the moulds. Stir in an airtight container.

CHEESE

No one is sure where and when cheese was first made, although its discovery was almost certainly an accident. The farmers of Mesopotamia domesticated sheep 10,000 years ago and wild cattle 8000 years ago; they are known to have made cheese from milk. The Greeks and Romans developed the idea by adding herbs and spices. During the middle ages, meat was hard to come by so cheese was used as a meat substitute, with cattle, sheep and goats kept for their milk rather than their meat.

At Huka Lodge we serve cheese after the main course and before the dessert, which is the correct way to incorporate cheese into a formal menu. We serve an endless array of savoury breads and loaves with the cheese, from plain bread to sundried tomato and olive bread. Often we serve a cheese selection instead of a sweet dessert.

Cheeses fall into several categories. Fresh cheese is eaten unripened. Soft cheese has been briefly ripened but still has a high moisture content. Semi hard cheese is matured cheese with less moisture. Hard cheese has been matured for a long period and has a very low moisture content. A cheese selection should contain cheeses from all these categories.

It is also important to have a variety of styles. Include soft white-rinded bries and camemberts along with full-bodied blue cheeses, cheddars and special herb or pepper coated cheeses.

Try to use cheeses made from different milks, such as sheep, goat and cow. There are others, such as yak milk cheese from China, camel milk cheese from Afghanistan and even donkey milk cheese from Iran, but these are not readily available.

Cheese must always be served at the correct degree of ripeness and at room temperature. It may be stored tightly wrapped in the refrigerator, but it must be removed at least 1 hour before being served.

Grapes, pears, dates, figs and apples accompany cheese nicely, along with cooked and raw vegetables, salad and, of course, wine.

CHOCOLATE

Cocoa is made from the seeds or beans of the Theobroma cacao *tree, which grows in the tropical American rain forests. It has been highly prized since the time of the Aztecs, when only those close to the king were allowed to drink the chocolate liquid made from cocoa.*

The Spanish brought the drink back to Spain in the sixteenth century and from there it spread through Europe. In 1657 the first chocolate shop was opened, not in France but in London.

The exact recipe for making chocolate is, in many cases, top secret. It is a blend of sugar, cocoa butter, spices and milk. The mixture is rolled and compressed and eventually becomes smooth and creamy, ready to be turned into the many shapes and sizes we are familiar with.

The quality of the finished product depends on the quality of the beans used.

CHOCOLATE CIGARS: Spread melted chocolate thinly over the back of a flat and smooth wooden tray. Place in the refrigerator and allow to set firm.

Take out of the refrigerator and stand ready with a metal spatula and a storage tray. Keep testing the curling quality of the chocolate as it warms to room temperature. As soon as the chocolate softens sufficiently to curl, hold the spatula at a slight angle and push along the tray to form a thin roll of chocolate.

If the chocolate becomes too soft return it to the refrigerator and begin the process again.

At Huka Lodge we use only good quality pure chocolate, which is a little more temperamental, but far superior to cooking chocolate, which is mainly vegetable fat and low in cocoa. The best type is dark, bitter chocolate, produced with cooking in mind. It is less sweet than eating chocolate, but it will melt more easily and can withstand higher temperatures. This chocolate should be warmed before use, as this will greatly improve its flavour.

Chop the chocolate quite finely and as evenly as possible, so that it will melt faster. Place in a bowl over a pot of hot water and stir until all the chocolate is completely melted. Remove from the heat.

Be careful not to allow any water into the chocolate as this will damage the texture, and do not overheat as this will also spoil the chocolate.

You may further process the chocolate by cooling half of it on a marble bench until it is thick and creamy, then returning it to the warm chocolate. Once mixed together and heated to 32°C (90°F) the chocolate will become far glossier.

CHOCOLATE FANS: Use the same process as for cigars, but this time push the metal spatula in a slight arc. Firmly hold one corner as you push and the chocolate will form into a fan shape.

CHOCOLATE WAFERS: You will need 8cm x 8cm (3″ x 3″) squares cut from a good quality shiny plastic carrier bag, and brioche moulds.

Melt the chocolate as above. Holding a plastic square by two corners, carefully lay on the melted chocolate. Do not allow the chocolate to flow over the top of the plastic. Carefully lift off the chocolate-coated plastic and shake a couple of times to allow excess to run off.

Lay the plastic chocolate-side up in a brioche mould so that a cup is formed. Be careful to avoid sharp kinks in the plastic as this will inhibit its removal.

Place in the refrigerator and allow to set firm. Carefully peel the plastic off the back of the chocolate, leaving the chocolate wafer basket. Keep your hands cold when peeling off the plastic by dipping them in iced water.

Store covered in the refrigerator.

ICE CREAM

Whether a simple, single flavour or a magnificent multi-flavoured bombe, ice cream has delighted generations of children and adults. With the invention of small domestic ice cream churns, the production of ice cream is well within the capability of anyone who cares to take a little time.

The base recipe and following flavour variations are those most relevant to this book, but our base recipe is very versatile. Make sure you have a suitable container chilling in the freezer.

INGREDIENTS — MAKES 1 LITRE (34 fl oz)

100g	(3½ oz)	castor sugar
3		egg yolks
250ml	(8½ fl oz)	milk
½		vanilla pod, split (for vanilla ice cream only)
250ml	(10 fl oz)	cream

METHOD: Whisk the sugar and egg yolks together until they turn pale yellow.

In a heavy-bottomed pot bring the milk to the boil with the vanilla pod. Once boiled remove the pod then pour the hot milk onto the egg yolk mixture, stirring as you pour.

Return the custard to the pot and place over a gentle heat. Cook to coating consistency, stirring constantly. Pass through a fine sieve into a clean bowl and cool. Lightly whip the cream then mix it into the custard.

When the custard is cold pour into a chilled ice cream churn and process until set. Transfer to the chilled container, cover and place in freezer.

BANANA ICE CREAM: Use the base recipe, but omit the vanilla pod. Once you have beaten the sugar and egg yolks together, mix in 75–100ml (2½–3½ fl oz) Bols crème de bananes. The liqueur will give the ice cream a distinctive banana flavour.

Crème de bananes is made from crushed bananas and sugar, steeped in spirit. It is also used in cocktails and other desserts.

ORANGE ICE CREAM: Use the base recipe, but omit the vanilla pod. Add the zest of an orange, very finely chopped, and 75ml (2½ fl oz) grand marnier to the whisked egg yolks and sugar.

Grand marnier is made from brandy and orange peel and is very versatile.

RUM AND RAISIN ICE CREAM: Use the base recipe, but omit the vanilla pod. Add 75ml (2½ fl oz) dark rum to the whisked egg yolks and sugar. Soak 75g (2½ oz) seedless raisins in warm water until soft. Drain and dry. Roughly chop the raisins then add to the cold custard just before you place it in the churn.

Rum is distilled from molasses. Colourless and dark varieties are available.

HONEY ICE CREAM: Use the base recipe, but omit the vanilla pod and replace the 100g (3½ oz) castor sugar with 3 tbsp runny honey and 50g (1½ oz) castor sugar.

CARAMEL ICE CREAM: Using a heavy-bottomed pot, caramelise 100g (3½ oz) sugar, stirring from time to time until a dark amber colour is achieved. Remove from the heat then carefully add 300ml (10 fl oz) cream a little at a time until it is all mixed in. If necessary return to a gentle heat to dissolve any pieces of toffee. Place aside but keep warm.

Make the custard with the eggs and milk as in the base recipe, but omit the vanilla. Beat the yolks until they are pale.

Mix the caramel into the warm custard well, then pass through a fine sieve into a clean bowl. Allow to completely cool.

Freeze as in base recipe.

SUGAR SYRUP

This general purpose syrup stores well, if covered in the refrigerator, and is very useful to have on hand as it is used in so many preparations.

A split vanilla pod may be added if a vanilla flavour is required. This recipe may safely be halved or doubled.

INGREDIENTS — MAKES ABOUT 800ml (27 fl oz)

400g	(14 oz)	castor sugar
600ml	(20 fl oz)	water

METHOD: Boil the sugar and water together for 1 minute in a heavy-bottomed pot. Pass through a fine sieve into a clean bowl. Allow to cool. Cover and keep in the refrigerator.

SPUN SUGAR

This is the sugar mixture we use in the preparation of sugar cages, sugar runouts and angel hair.

If you use a sugar thermometer, then sugar should be boiled to 'hard crack', which is 150–158°C (300–315°F). If you do not use a thermometer, the mixture must be golden brown. You can test for 'hard crack' by dipping a cold spoon into the syrup then into cold water. If the cooled sugar on the spoon is still pliable, continue to boil. If the cooled sugar is hard and cracks like glass then it is ready. This happens in a matter of seconds, so test regularly.

INGREDIENTS

350g	(12½ oz)	castor sugar
2 tbsp		liquid glucose
100ml	(3½ fl oz)	water

METHOD: Place the ingredients in a heavy-bottomed pot. Gently melt the sugar over a medium heat. Once the liquid is clear, boil to 'hard crack'. Remove the pot from the heat and if necessary plunge it briefly into a sink of iced water to stop it cooking.

SUGAR CAGES: Lightly oil the back of a ladle. Using a dessert spoon, take a spoonful of the hot syrup. Allow the syrup to drip off the spoon until a constant thread is formed. Quickly criss-cross the oiled ladle with a continuous thread, forming a web. Finally, wind the thread around the base of the ladle several times to form a base. Trim off any hanging threads with a pair of scissors, then carefully lift the cage off the ladle.

The cages will keep for some time if kept cool, dry and airtight. Do not refrigerate.

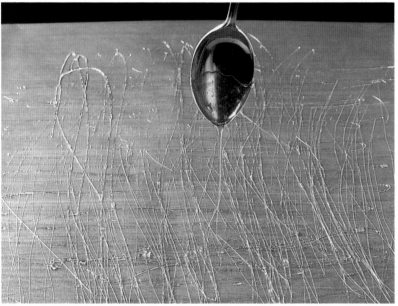

SUGAR RUNOUTS: Oil a flat baking tray then follow the same process as above, but flicking the thread backwards and forwards across the baking tray. Allow to set then break off pieces for placing on desserts.

ANGEL HAIR: Dip a fork or small whisk into the syrup then rapidly flick backwards and forwards over a rolling pin or broom handle suspended between two chairs, over newspaper. Once the set threads have reasonably covered the surface, carefully gather them up and store on a lightly oiled baking tray or in an airtight container.

This type of spun sugar is very delicate and must be kept dry and airtight if not for immediate use.

QUICK AND EASY SPONGES

There are several ways of preparing light and tasty sponges. Some, such as genoese, are lightly flavoured with lemon zest and made moist and rich with the addition of melted butter.

Many of our desserts that require sponge, such as the charlottes and grape flan, use a basic preparation that will take on other flavours if required, but remain neutral when need be.

The following two variations are very simple in their preparation. You will need a 24–25cm (9½–10″) cake tin, spring-form if possible.

PLAIN SPONGE

INGREDIENTS

6	eggs
170g (6 oz)	castor sugar
120g (4¼ oz)	flour
4 tbsp	cornflour

METHOD: Place the eggs and sugar in a large mixing bowl. Whisk at a high speed until light and fluffy and doubled in quantity. This can be done cold or over a bowl of simmering water. If done warm the sabayon will be a little more durable as the eggs will have been slightly cooked.

Sift the flour and cornflour together, then sprinkle over the sabayon. Very carefully fold into the egg mixture using a large metal spoon. This may be done using a whisk, although there is a danger of over whisking and knocking too much air from the mixture.

Brush the cake tin with melted butter then dust with flour. Shake off excess flour. Pour the sponge mixture into the tin.

Place in a preheated 190°C (375°F) oven for 35–40 minutes, with the fan on. Once baked cool slightly then remove from the tin and place on a cake rack.

CHOCOLATE SPONGE

INGREDIENTS

6	eggs
170g (6 oz)	castor sugar
120g (4¼ oz)	flour
1½ tbsp	cornflour
4 tbsp	cocoa

METHOD: Follow the same process as with the plain sponge, but add the cocoa with the flour and cornflour.

PÂTE SABLÉE
(SWEET SHORTBREAD PASTRY)

Sablée is the French word for sandy, an adequate description of this delicate, light and crumbly pastry. Sablée is superb as a crust for lemon tarts or served as little biscuits with fresh berries.

Like any pastry with a high butter and egg content, pâte sablée must not be over kneaded or it will become greasy and elastic. Too much handling will damage the pastry as the heat and oils from your hands begin to break down the very delicate structure.

Well covered, pâte sablée will keep for a week in the refrigerator, but it does not freeze very well.

Store in conveniently sized pieces or rolled into a cylinder; because of the high butter content it will become quite hard in the refrigerator.

METHOD: Cut the butter into small pieces, place in a bowl and work with your fingers until soft.

Sift the icing sugar then mix it into the butter along with a pinch of salt. Carefully add the egg yolks and mix well.

A little at a time, mix in the flour until it is all incorporated. Place on a lightly dusted work surface and knead with your hand three or four times only. Roll into a cylinder, wrap in plastic wrap and store in the refrigerator.

If you are going to use the pastry the same day, allow it to rest in the refrigerator for at least 1 hour.

NOTE: When using pâte sablée, be quick working with it as the pastry softens quickly and becomes very hard to handle.

INGREDIENTS — MAKES 575g

200g (7 oz)	soft, unsalted butter
100g (3½ oz)	icing sugar
	pinch of salt
2	egg yolks
250g (9 oz)	standard flour

CHOCOLATE SABLÉ

METHOD: Follow the same instructions as for pâte sablée, adding the sieved cocoa to the flour.

INGREDIENTS

200g (7 oz)	soft, unsalted butter
100g (3½ oz)	icing sugar
	pinch of salt
2	egg yolks
200g (7 oz)	flour
50g (1½ oz)	cocoa

GLOSSARY

ACIDULATE: To add a little lemon juice or vinegar to prevent discoloration.

BAIN-MARIE: A water bath, made by either placing a bowl over a pot of simmering water or, for the oven, a cake tin in a roasting tin half-filled with water.

BAKE BLIND: To cook an empty pastry case, lined with greaseproof paper and half-filled with beans or rice, until barely done.

COATING CONSISTENCY: The state a mixture reaches when it will coat the back of a wooden spoon.

COUVERTURE: A waxy form of chocolate that can be bought in bulk, making it a high-quality cheaper substitute for dessert chocolate.

DARIOLE MOULD: A small, cylindrical mould with sloping sides, used for making individual desserts.

FLAMBÉ: Food drenched in alcohol and then lit.

FRITURE: Fat in which food is fried.

GANACHE: A chocolate and cream paste used for filling cakes and pastries, and ideal for piping onto poached fruits.

JULIENNE: Food cut into fine strips.

PÂTE SABLÉE: A delicate sweet shortbread pastry.

QUENELLE: Mousse, cream or ganache formed into a barrel shape with two spoons.

RAMEKIN: A small round china dish used for individual servings.

SABAYON: Mixture comprising sugar and eggs.

SABLÉ BISCUIT: A biscuit made of pâte sablée.

SAVARIN MOULD: A ring mould with a rounded top.

TUILE: A type of wafer which, when baked, is bent over to resemble a curved tile.

INDEX

A

Apple:

    Apple crumble with blackberries and cream, 94

    Apple fritters with calvados sorbet, 48

    Calvados creams with caramelised apple and syrup, 72

    Fig and apple compôte with frangelico sauce and walnut sticks, 40

    Orange flavoured waffles with apple compôte and apple syrup, 102

    Stuffed apples with sablé and crème anglaise, 77

    Vanilla bavarois with apple purée and chocolate ganache, 90

Apricot:

    Apricot crème brûlée, 62

    Apricot glaze, 46

B

Banana:

    Banana muffins, 126

    Savarins with banana ice cream and sautéed banana, 56

Bavarois:

    Vanilla bavarois with apple purée and chocolate ganache, 90

Berries, mixed:

    Crème de cassis mousse with red berry compôte and sablé leaves, 36

    Mulled wine berries topped with port and orange granité, 39

    Summer berry feuilleté with sabayon, 89

    Warm summer berries gratinated with caramel sabayon, served with rum and raisin ice cream and orange tuiles, 82

Blackberry:

    Apple crumble with blackberries and cream, 94

    Fruit flan, 46

Black bun with ginger sauce, 84

Blueberry:

    Blueberry tarte with sabra syrup, 70

    Summer berry feuilleté with sabayon, 89

Boiled fruit puddings with spiced prunes and amaretto crème anglaise, 118

Bread and butter pudding, 43

C

Cakes, **see also** Gâteau:

    Black bun with ginger sauce, 84

    Fruit cake, 60

    Lemon verbena cake with tequila and lime syrup, 106

    Stollen, 123

    Whiskey cake with coffee sauce, 30

Calvados creams with caramelised apple and syrup, 72

Caramel ice cream over dark and white chocolate sauces, 38

Caramelised pear tarte, 92

Caramelised pumpkin terrine with vanilla ice cream, 54

Caramelised rice pudding with tropical fruit and passionfruit sauce, 26

Cheese, 128

Cheesecake:

    Rum and raisin cheesecake, 88

Cherries with snow eggs, 49

Chestnut cream, 42

Chocolate, to make, 130

    Chocolate and rice pudding, 44

    Chocolate marquise wrapped in tuile, 28

    Chocolate mousse with sponge fingers and scalded orange sauce, 64

    Choclate sablé, 137

    Chocolate sablé with raspberries, 98

    Chocolate sponge, 136

    Chocolate terrine with roast pears and a nut crust, 50

    Chocolate truffle tarte, 78

    Cigars, 130

    Fans, 131

    Hazelnut Saxony pudding with warm chocolate sauce, 86

    Wafers, 131

Compôtes:

    Apple, 102

    Compôte of dried fruits baked under a cinnamon sponge, 32

    Fig and apple compôte with frangelico sauce and walnut sticks, 40

    Red berry, 36

Coulis, raspberry, 98

Creams:

    Calvados creams with caramelised apple and syrup, 72

    Chestnut, 42

    Frangelico liqueur, 74

    Grape liqueur, 86

    Lemon and wine, 116

Crème anglaise, 78, 98

    Amaretto, 118

    Honey, 112

Crème brûlée, apricot, 62

Crème de cassis mousse with red berry compôte and sablé leaves, 36

Crème pâtissière, 46

Crêpes:

    Kiwifruit crêpe soufflé, 108

D

Date:

    Date and walnut loaf, 124

    Date muffins, 125

Dried fruit:

    Compôte of dried fruits baked under a cinnamon sponge, 32

    Dried fruit loaf, 124

F

Feuilleté:

    Summer berry feuilleté with sabayon, 89

    Fig and apple compôte with frangelico sauce and walnut sticks, 40

Flans:

    Fruit flan, 46

    Grape liqueur flan with sauternes glaze, 86

    Mixed nut flan, 52

Fritters:

    Apple fritters with calvados sorbet, 48

    Leche frita, 95

Fruit, **see also** Apple, Apricot, etc:

    Caramelised rice pudding with tropical fruit and passionfruit sauce, 26

    Selection, 127

Fruit cake, 60

    Black bun with ginger sauce, 84

Fruit flan, 46

G

Ganache, chocolate, 30, 90

Gâteau:

    Hazelnut gâteau filled with frangelico liqueur cream, 74

Glazes:

    Apricot, 46

    Red wine, 96

    Sauternes, 86

Granité, port and orange, 39

Grape liqueur flan with sauternes glaze, 86

H

Hazelnut gâteau filled with frangelico liqueur cream, 74

Hazelnut Saxony pudding with warm chocolate sauce, 76

I

Ice cream, to make, 132

    Banana, 132

    Caramel, 132

    Caramel ice cream over dark and white chocolate sauces, 38

    Caramelised pumpkin terrine with vanilla ice cream, 54

Honey, 132

Meringue nests with chestnut cream, vanilla ice cream and plum purée, 42

Orange, 132

Pears caramelised in honey with vanilla ice cream and sabayon, 114

Savarins with banana ice cream and sautéed banana, 56

Rum and raisin, 82, 132

Whole roast pears with ice cream and chocolate sauce, 34

K

Kiwifruit crêpe soufflé, 108

L

Leche frita, 95

Lemon:

    Lemon and praline syllabub with nougatine shapes, 33

    Lemon and wine cream, 116

    Lemon meringue pie, 110

    Lemon soufflé with lemon butter sauce, 80

    Lemon verbena cake with tequila and lime syrup, 106

Lime and buttermilk tarte with lemon and wine cream, 116

Liqueur creams:

    Frangelico, 74

    Grape, 86

Loaves:

    Date and walnut, 124

    Dried fruit, 124

M

Marinated strawberry terrine with lime syrup, 53

Marquise:

    Chocolate marquise wrapped in tuile, 28

Melon:

    Orange and champagne timbale with melon purée, 63

Meringue:

    Lemon meringue pie, 110

    Meringue nests with chestnut cream, vanilla ice cream and plum purée, 42

    Pavlova sandwich with caramel sauce, 100

Mixed nut flan, 52

Mousses:

    Chocolate mousse with sponge fingers and scalded orange sauce, 64

    Crème de cassis mousse with red berry compôte and sablé leaves, 36

    Pear mousse with ginger and cocoa sabayon, 58

    Rhubarb mousse over honey crème anglaise, 112

Muffins:

    Banana, 126